YOUR
WEDDING,
YOUR
WAY

YOUR WEDDING, YOUR WAY

INSPIRATION & IDEAS

TIPS & TIMELINES

DESTINATION ELOPEMENTS, INTIMATE CEREMONIES, AND OTHER NONTRADITIONAL NUPTIALS

CHRONICLE BOOKS
SAN FRANCISCO

KIM OLSEN & SCOTT SHAW

TO OUR PARTNERS:

*Kurtis, for trusting the process,
and Camille, who knew what she wanted.*

LIBRARY OF CONGRESS CATALOGING-IN-PUBLICATION DATA

NAMES: OLSEN, KIM (KIMBERLY ELAINE), AUTHOR. | SHAW, SCOTT, 1960- AUTHOR. | GUL, MARIA INES, ILLUSTRATOR. TITLE: YOUR WEDDING, YOUR WAY : DESTINATION ELOPEMENTS, INTIMATE CEREMONIES, AND OTHER NONTRADITIONAL NUPTIALS / KIM OLSEN & SCOTT SHAW ; [ILLUSTRATIONS BY] MARIA INES GUL. DESCRIPTION: SAN FRANCISCO : CHRONICLE BOOKS, [2021] | "A GUIDE FOR THE MODERN COUPLE"--TITLE PAGE. IDENTIFIERS: LCCN 2021021003 | ISBN 9781797202990 (HARDCOVER) SUBJECTS: LCSH: WEDDINGS. | ELOPEMENT. CLASSIFICATION: LCC HQ745 .O47 2021 | DDC 392.5--DC23 LC RECORD AVAILABLE AT HTTPS://LCCN.LOC.GOV/2021021003

MANUFACTURED IN CHINA.

DESIGN BY RACHEL HARRELL.

TYPESETTING BY HOWIE SEVERSON.

10 9 8 7 6 5 4 3 2 1

CHRONICLE BOOKS AND GIFTS ARE AVAILABLE AT SPECIAL QUANTITY DISCOUNTS TO CORPORATIONS, PROFESSIONAL ASSOCIATIONS, LITERACY PROGRAMS, AND OTHER ORGANIZATIONS. FOR DETAILS AND DISCOUNT INFORMATION, PLEASE CONTACT OUR PREMIUMS DEPARTMENT AT CORPORATESALES@CHRONICLEBOOKS.COM OR AT 1-800-759-0190.

CHRONICLE BOOKS LLC
680 SECOND STREET
SAN FRANCISCO, CALIFORNIA 94107
WWW.CHRONICLEBOOKS.COM

Contents

Intr

oduction

The bride and groom sit side by side at a long wooden table. Pine branches run down its center, anchoring a scatter of twinkling mercury glass votives and two floral centerpieces bursting with crimson and peach roses. Servers hover, pouring Champagne.

Soon, the three-course menu inspired by "Adirondack ambience" will be served to the dinner party of eleven close family members and friends: a first course option of pan-seared sea scallops or seasonal salad; the second of pan-seared halibut, venison, or steak tenderloin; and the third, a small, two-tiered, maple rosemary cake with fresh blackberries. At the far end of the table, a stone fireplace for roasting marshmallows stretches from the floor to the ceiling like a proud, quiet host. Outside, January snow rests on Lake Placid.

The newlyweds, Amber and Bryan, had exchanged vows earlier that day in a sun-drenched room overlooking the lake where Amber, wearing a white silk dress with a hand-embroidered train, a delicate diamond crown, and no veil, walked down the aisle on her father's arm. Lake Placid was a frequent weekend getaway for Amber and Bryan while dating, a place brimming with memories and sentiment, perfect for their elopement.

They'd been dating for seven years when Bryan proposed in a hammock in Maui at sunset, and neither wanted a long, drawn-out engagement followed by a big wedding bash. But more than that, they wanted to make their wedding day personal to *them*. "Conventional weddings can be so overwhelmingly complicated that all of the savory little details get easily lost in the shuffle," says Bryan. "What we created was a day where we could truly take our time, drink in the moment, and share the best day of our lives with the people closest to us.

"People ask us all the time, 'You think you'll ever look back and wish you had a big wedding?' The answer is still an emphatic and resounding, 'No way.'"

Amber and Bryan are certainly not alone at the communal table. Google searches for "elope" are at an all-time high, and "elopement photography" is among the top ten wedding search terms on Pinterest, where inspiration for wedding dresses, tablescapes, and escort cards is born. But why? Why are elopements, intimate ceremonies, and nontraditional weddings suddenly so popular? How did we get to a place where a couple (so many couples) would rather say their vows on a mountaintop than in a room full of one hundred fifty people?

As a journalist, I love digging into questions like these. And as a millennial—the generation leading the shift in what is considered an elopement—I can relate. I experienced the economic effects of the 2008 recession and have a decent chunk of student loan debt, making the thought of dropping $30,000 on one day highly unappealing (this is in US dollars, which are used for all costs in the book).

In 2020, I watched the COVID-19 pandemic steamroll through wedding season, canceling weddings worldwide and forcing couples to majorly trim their guest lists. It also brought to the forefront what really matters on a wedding day (turns out, many couples were happy to part with the planning).

Yet I understand that weddings are deeply important for some families, and many couples not only have the means to cover them financially, but also genuinely *want* to spend their money on a big celebration. I just have personally never had that urge. I don't like being the center of attention, and the idea of selecting bridesmaids and having them endure months of group texts about *my wedding* sounds, quite frankly, terrible. Suffice it to say, the idea of eloping naturally fits in my wheelhouse.

To figure out why this trend was growing and morphing into far more than just the courthouse ceremony, I started by looking at the literal definition of "elope." Hundreds of years ago, when the word was first used circa 1593, it had a distinct meaning: to leave one's spouse for a lover. This definition likely came about due to the fact that many (teenage) marriages were arranged, so the only way to live happily ever after was to secretly run away with someone you actually loved, à la Romeo and Juliet. By the seventeenth century, "elope" had come to mean "to run away with a romantic interest," which is what most people think of when they hear the word today.

But the definition has continued to evolve. The wordsmiths over at Merriam-Webster have shared that the meaning of "elope" is "shifting toward a small destination wedding." They also say that it means one that isn't "financially insane," or lets you eliminate guests you "would rather not invite," both of which are funny—and true. Overall, they acknowledge that the changing definition is just part of the journey of language and ask, "Can you accept that? We do."

I do too. I've interviewed dozens of couples who defined elopement on their own terms in order to gain insight on why and how they did it. One couple turned the annual family vacation to St. Simons Island into their wedding celebration; it was the bride's second marriage, and she wanted it to be nothing like her big, traditional first wedding. Another had a true elopement—just the two of them and a photographer—to Florence, where they had fallen in love while studying abroad. They chose to do it this way simply because they live a quiet life and never even considered having a larger affair. Others had engagement parties-turned-surprise-ceremonies, just to flip the script.

Overall, couples' reasons for eloping or having an intimate wedding fell into three main buckets (aside from the pandemic, which is covered in chapter 11): to save money; not wanting to be the center of attention; or wishing to avoid (or halt) the stress of wedding planning. Stress was ultimately the biggest reason—one heavily supported, interestingly enough, by a survey from Zola, a company whose business model relies on couples to plan big weddings and register for things ranging from KitchenAid mixers to dog-walking services to airline gift cards. The survey found that out of five hundred engaged or newly married couples, 96 percent said wedding planning was stressful, and 55 percent considered eloping or calling the whole thing off.

Calling the whole thing off.

The survey also mentions that 86 percent of respondents suffered, on average, more than three stress-induced symptoms, including skin breakouts, hair loss, loss of sex drive, insomnia, and headaches. All from planning what is essentially a fancy event.

If you feel like you're heading down the path toward no sleep and hair loss, or want to avoid it from the start, this book will help guide and shape your wedding day into one that is truly special and unique, done your way. Throughout, I use the word "elopement" to refer to *all* forms of nontraditional weddings, not just running off to Bali. It's divided into eleven chapters, starting with two on the logistics of planning an elopement and navigating the world of vendors, followed by nine chapters that focus on a different way to go about it, with a couple's story in each. I've also included time lines, checklists, tips, and how-tos. It's a useful resource that's fun too. Because that's what it's really about: truly enjoying your day.

And, as my landlord—who got married in a law office above a Chipotle—puts it, "It's about the love, not the fluff."

Cheers to love, and to celebrating it your way.

CHAPTER 1

The Bluepri

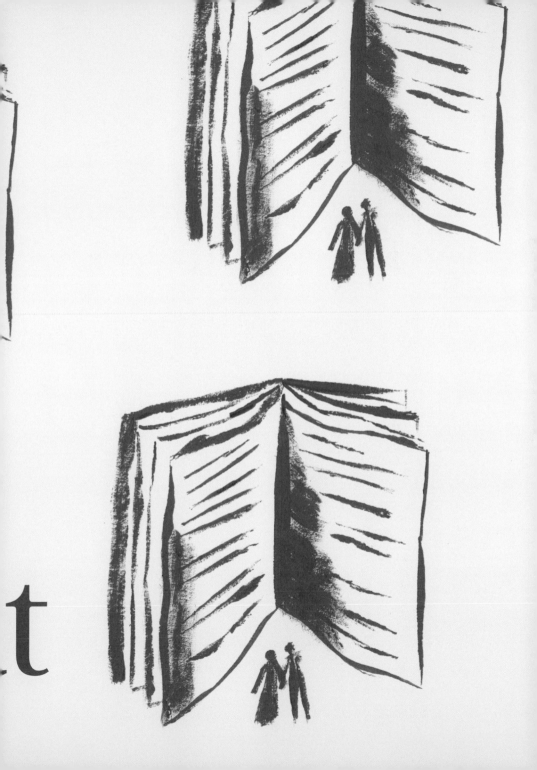

Lauren & Lindsay

"If I told you that Lindsay and I eloped, would you believe me?"

So begins a caption on Instagram that Lauren wrote one year to the day after she and her now-husband, Lindsay, stood in a civil celebrant's living room, facing each other and clasping hands. The lights were dimmed, and outside it was dumping cold February rain. They looked at each other and thought, *This wasn't supposed to happen like this.*

What was supposed to happen was they would marry on a sweeping estate with a grand staircase seemingly built for wedding portraits. She'd get ready with a glam squad and wear an elegant white robe as she popped Champagne with her bridesmaids. Her father would walk her down the aisle of a garden on the estate's grounds, her 120-inch [3 m] cathedral-length veil trailing behind her. At the reception, Lindsay would scoop her up and her strapless satin gown would billow around them.

Instead, seven months ahead of their planned wedding date, they stood in a stranger's living room and were legally married with no witnesses. Lauren wore a white blazer. There were no rings. "We wanted it to be as transactional as possible," says Lauren. They went home and had their first dance in their kitchen to the song they had picked out for their "real" wedding, "Let It Be Me" by Ray LaMontagne: "When all your faith is gone / And it feels like you can't go on / Let it be me."

Lindsay, a native of Australia, had come to the United States in 2016 on a special work visa called the L1A visa. This visa allows overseas companies to transfer executives and managers for a temporary stay, and it cannot be transferred to another employer.

Around four months after arriving in the United States, Lindsay met Lauren on Tinder. On their first date at a corner pizza bistro, they closed down the restaurant, then went to a place nearby for dessert and closed that down too. Early in their relationship, they joked about getting married at the courthouse or applying to be on the show *90 Day Fiancé*, which would—jokes aside—ensure that Lindsay was safe to stay In the United States for good.

"Thinking back, we didn't really talk about it being an issue, because we figured that by the time his visa was going to run out through work, we would be married, and he could go the green card route," says Lauren, reiterating, "we really didn't think it was going to be an issue."

Then, in late 2018, just after Lindsay and Lauren got engaged and were planning their wedding, his situation at work became unstable. The company he'd been with for more than eight years, and had received numerous awards from in Australia, was, in the United States, threatening to fire him. But according to the terms of the L1A visa, he couldn't switch companies. He was essentially trapped. And if he were to be terminated,

he would have to leave the country within twenty-four hours per the terms of the visa.

One day in early February 2019, Lindsay texted Lauren, seemingly out of the blue. He told her he thought they needed to get legally married sooner than their planned September wedding, "which didn't go over well," says Lauren. By that point, they had hired the venue, photographer, and videographer. She'd ordered her wedding dress. "The last thing I ever thought I would do is elope."

But she knew it was the right, realistic, responsible thing to do. Their county courthouse doesn't hold civil ceremonies, so they found a civil celebrant on the county clerk's website and, a week later, eloped in her living room.

On her social media post a year later—which is how they broke the news that they had secretly eloped to *everyone*, including immediate family—she explained: "The main reason we decided to share this is to shed some light on the US immigration process. Most people think that once you are married, you have a green card and can work automatically. No." Until you file a green card application, nothing changes.

Lauren and Lindsay hired an immigration lawyer to guide them through the process. If you make any mistakes on the paperwork, your application is canceled and you lose the money it cost to apply: $1,200 for the actual green card, and $600 for a physical, vaccinations, and fingerprints. The lawyer cost $2,500. Lauren had to prove that she could support them both to ensure that Lindsay wouldn't go on government assistance programs should he lose his job. If this were to happen, his green card application would get canceled, given the conditions of his work visa.

It took five months for Lindsay to receive his temporary Employment Authorization Document (EAD), which allowed him to leave his job and work anywhere in the United States. "When he opened it up in the mail, we were jumping up and down," says Lauren. "It felt like we were safe now. Something with so much power to upheave our lives seemed so easy and quick once it was done."

The EAD arrived exactly one week before the wedding they had been planning for nearly a year was to take place. And take place it did. Lindsay's family flew in from Australia. Lauren got her glam squad and popped Champagne surrounded by her bridesmaids. Her father walked her down the aisle in the formal garden of Airlie, a countryside estate in Northern Virginia, where Martin Luther King Jr. once hosted civil rights meetings. At the end of the ceremony, as Lauren and Lindsay walked down the aisle as husband and wife, guests cheered and waved small Australian flags. In a black-and-white photo from the reception that Lauren posted on their one-month anniversary, her arms are wrapped tightly around Lindsay's neck as he lifts her off the ground, her dress a blurry cascade of satin.

Lauren & Lindsay's Fine Print

LIVE: Springfield, Virginia

WORK: Lauren is the director of culture and inclusion at Enabled Intelligence, and Lindsay is director of recruitment at 11th Hour Service.

AGES WHEN THEY ELOPED: They were both thirty-three.

LAUREN'S FIRST IMPRESSION: "He was genuine, funny, handsome, and we had so much in common. Not just interests but what we wanted out of life . . . family, house, dog. I was laughing the entire first date and could just tell that he was a good person. After all the messed-up guys I had dated in the past, something as basic as finding a good person became a top priority on my list."

LINDSAY'S FIRST IMPRESSION: "She looked very strong, powerful, not ditzy, well looked after, there for a reason, very attractive. Better looking in person than in her photos. She was very direct and was asking me questions with intent (to find out if I was right for her) versus just fluffy small talk questions. Luckily my answers were in line with what she wanted to hear. I was very nervous but also comfortable. I knew that I needed someone in my life who was strong and could lead in a relationship and push things forward."

RELATIONSHIP TIME LINE: Dated for two years → Engaged for four months → Eloped February 2019 → "Real" wedding September 2019 → Honeymooned November 2019

PROPOSAL: Says Lauren: "We had a trip planned to the Outer Banks in North Carolina, which is my happy place. I grew up going there every summer with my family. We were going with my brother and his wife and my sister-in-law and her now fiancé. We call this group "sibs & sigs"—siblings and significant others. We agreed that we would go down to the

beach to take some photos before we went out to dinner. We started with family photos of my brother, his wife, Katie, and their dog, Kona, for their Christmas card. This was a decoy. We switched and it was Lindsay and my turn to take photos. We walked to the photo spot and boom, Lindsay dropped to one knee, I took like three steps backward and covered my face. Lindsay knew the two things I cared about in regard to a proposal were that it was a surprise and that we got really good photos. We ended up not getting professional engagement photos done because we had a little session right there on the beach."

WEDDING VENUE: Civil celebrant's living room

DISTANCE FROM HOME TO VENUE: 6.5 miles / 10.5 km

NUMBER OF GUESTS: 0

SHE WORE: White blazer from H&M and black leggings

HE WORE: Burgundy sweater from Old Navy and jeans

RINGS: Lindsay had Lauren's engagement ring, a thin yellow gold band with a solitaire stone, custom made.

SPENT: $80

Welcome to the Blueprint

Welcome to your blueprint for eloping, no matter where you go, what you wear, or who you tell. You're a cool couple, not a regular couple, and we're here to shake things up with you. Read on for everything you need to know as you begin to plan your elopement, whether it's shaping up to be a hometown dinner party-slash-staycation, a misty mountaintop trek, or a passport-required excursion to somewhere with turquoise water and personal butlers. Nowadays, anything goes, as long as it's decidedly *you*.

First Up: Choose Your Destination

Choosing a destination is the most crucial part of planning your elopement. It shapes the foundation from which every ensuing decision is made: your date, guest list, budget, travel arrangements, and, well, shoes, to start.

The good news is that unlike with a larger wedding, you aren't (as) bound by a budget or guest list, meaning you can focus more on making your elopement a reflection of your personalities and interests. If you're outdoorsy, that might mean shacking up in a cabin in the Smoky Mountains and hiking to a viewpoint for your ceremony. Urbanites might embrace a killer hotel rooftop at sunset and then treat themselves to the presidential suite for their first night as newlyweds. Maybe you're both foodies, so an Italian elopement capped with a pasta-making class is the kind of food coma experience you're looking for.

And the cool thing about eloping— among 1,539,822 others—is that you don't have to venue shop (unless you want to). While most weddings take place at an event-ready venue, elopements are often about a simple location—a beach, waterfall, cliffside, and so on. The limitations that come with working with a venue are replaced with a lot more freedom and flexibility. Need to change your date from a Saturday to a Sunday a week out? Chances are that sunflower field will still be available.

Just remember: Eloping doesn't have to require hopping on a plane, so there's no need to get overwhelmed by all the options from around the world thanks to Instagram. (A friendly heads-up—a lot of those ethereal, perfectly lit, are-they-gonna-fall-off-that-cliff photos are really just staged photoshoots. Now you know why everyone is so tan and glittery.) Many couples opt for something low-key and low stress, choosing to elope to a local spot that holds special meaning to them, such as the restaurant where they had their first date or the park where they got engaged. And of course, there's always the courthouse, for those who truly are looking to keep their wedding easy, fast, and simple.

Getting There

Do a deep dive into precisely how to get to your location, especially if you're including witnesses or inviting guests. This could be as simple as knowing that the lodge you're eloping to is on a toll road, so let guests know to bring cash. Island destinations might require a ferry ride—for your guests *and*

their rental cars. If you're planning to ask your guests to walk or hike to the ceremony, ensure they're all fully capable of doing so and dressed appropriately, including footwear.

Also, keep your vendors in mind as you plan. Your photographer will be hauling equipment, so if your wedding is outdoors or in a remote locale, be sure to have a conversation about where and how far they are willing to trek.

For yourselves, be realistic about what you're able to carry too, regarding attire, flowers, and any celebratory libations. Sure, you want that shot of your veil soaring in the wind on an oceanfront cliff. Just make sure it's packed in a garment bag that you're willing to carry as you hike there, and that someone can help you put it on once you're at the spot. Fortunately, many elopement photographers are experienced in doing this.

Pick a Date

The bottom line when choosing a date is to be flexible. Many venues that cater to elopements allow them only on specific weekdays and during specific hours (and even certain months). These venues also usually do big weddings on weekends, so don't set your heart on a Saturday in October (which has replaced June as the most popular month to get married). The same goes when researching vendors, many of whom also do weekend weddings and may only be available on weekdays.

But know that you might get lucky—some venues end up empty on weekends around holidays such as the Fourth of July and Labor Day, so ask if you can put your name on a "wait list" of sorts in the instance those Saturdays open up. Venues would rather host an intimate ceremony than no ceremony at all.

If your elopement involves any sort of travel, research the best times of year to visit your chosen destination, weather-wise. Along with the local forecast, get familiar with when natural disasters such as hurricanes, tsunamis, and polar vortexes tend to strike. Look for outliers as well—just because it's April and balmy in Philadelphia doesn't mean it isn't snowing in Chicago.

One decision to give some thought to is which date will be your anniversary: the date you say "I do" or the date you sign your marriage license. Some couples opt for the former, which is decidedly more romantic, and some celebrate both, because really, there are no rules.

FOLKLORE FUN

Does your decision-making rely heavily on your daily horoscope and finding pennies faceup? Here's some folklore to help you decide on which day of the week to elope, courtesy of *Every Woman's Encyclopaedia*, published in 1910:

"Monday for wealth,
Tuesday for health,
Wednesday the best day of all,
Thursday for losses,
Friday for crosses,
and Saturday no luck at all."

As for Sunday, it was once *the day* for weddings in Elizabethan times, as it was the only day people had off from work. However, the Puritans put a stop to it in the 1600s, believing one should not do anything resembling fun on the Sabbath.

And, if your belief system aligns with the above, you might want to consider the time of day you get married as well. Chinese tradition says to get married on the half-hour mark, when the minute hand is rising from six to twelve, which signifies good luck.

According to Southern folklore, if an engaged couple wants to ensure good weather on their big day, they need to bury a bottle of bourbon at the ceremony site exactly one month prior to the ceremony. On the day of the wedding, the bottle is dug up and served at the reception. While highly impractical for destination elopements—unless you've hired a vendor near the location who will kindly bury the booze for you—it might be something fun to incorporate into a local elopement, as long as you have permission from the property owner, it's your own backyard, or you aren't breaking any laws.

The Four Types of Ceremonies

Civil

A civil ceremony is performed by a legal official such as a judge or county clerk, or someone who's gone through the formal training to become an officiant. These are nonreligious ceremonies, and you're free to write your own vows, but be sure to check the specific requirements with the county clerk's office where you're marrying, as these do vary by location. (And FYI, civil ceremonies don't have to take place in a courthouse—they can happen pretty much anywhere it's legal to get married.)

The word "officiant" originally referred to a member of the clergy, such as a priest or rabbi, who performed a legal marriage. Nowadays, it's common to use the term to refer to any person who performs the role of officiating a legal marriage ceremony.

Religious

Religious ceremonies take place in a house of worship and are performed by a minister, rabbi, or priest. These are the most rigid of the four kinds of ceremonies, as they follow a formulaic order of events that's not likely to change. Religious ceremonies are often deeply moving to those strongly rooted in their faith.

Spiritual

The newest kid on the scene, spiritual ceremonies are increasingly popular as they allow couples to merge their own spiritual backgrounds and beliefs outside of the confines and rules of a house of worship. These work well for couples with different religious or ethnic backgrounds because the couple can write their own vows while weaving their own rituals, customs, and beliefs into the ceremony.

Nearly a third of Americans today identify as spiritual, not religious.

Symbolic

If you're deep in Instagram #destinationelopements, chances are you're ogling a slew of symbolic—not legal—ceremonies. These are very common abroad, as most countries have strict policies around marriage, especially when it comes to foreigners. The easiest thing to do is to tie the knot in a legal ceremony at home, then head to your destination for a romantic, intimate, and highly photogenic celebration of commitment. Or flip it, and do your symbolic ceremony abroad, then make things legal when you return home.

Brush Up on the Marriage Laws

Regardless of what type of ceremony you choose, don't overlook some hugely important fine print: the marriage laws for your destination. Because marriage and the government are not mutually exclusive, it's crucial to familiarize yourself with the laws wherever you're hoping to make this thing legal.

In the United States, laws regarding the waiting period, age requirement, and number of witnesses vary by state. The best way to get the official, most up-to-date information is to check the website for the *county* you're getting married in, as well as the state.

> Your marriage license gets filed in the state—specifically, the county—you get married in, not the state you reside in. This applies to all fifty states. And to clear up a ton of confusion, you don't need to be a resident of the state in which you're eloping in order to get married there.

The Paperwork in Seven Easy Steps

A marriage application is not a marriage license. A marriage license is not a marriage certificate. A marriage certificate is not a . . . You get it. Read on for a breakdown of each.

1. When you're ready to start the process of going from fiancés to spouses, the first thing to do is fill out the marriage application. If

your state and/or county permits, you can fill out the application online on the county clerk's website (some courthouses, especially the highly busy ones, such as Las Vegas, prefer this in order to speed things up). However, many courthouses require you to apply in person together. If this is the case, you'll need to arrive with the proper forms of identification (current driver's license, government-issued ID, passport, or an original birth certificate or a certified copy of it) along with money for the application fee. Brush up on which forms of payment are accepted before you go too, as some courthouses still only deal in cash.

2. Next, go home and wait out the waiting period, if there is one, for the county you applied in. Theoretically, this chunk of time is for couples to deeply think about whether they want to go through with the marriage. If there are any reservations, now would probably be the best time to have a big talk.

3. Once the waiting period is over, you can either pick up your marriage license or have it mailed to you (in some states, a trusted third party can pick it up on your behalf). Here, it's vital to know how long the marriage license is valid for before it expires, which varies broadly by state; for instance, in Virginia the license expires after sixty days, in Arizona it's good for a year, and in Mississippi it never expires. Knowing the expiration date is critical when planning an elopement, particularly if it involves extensive travel or vendors. In many states, the marriage license is only good for thirty days, meaning you'd better have your officiant, any witnesses, and any vendors lined up once that license hits your hands.

4. Go get married. *Do not forget to take your marriage license with you.* If you forget to bring it, the marriage cannot be legally performed by your officiant (if they do so, it's considered a misdemeanor).

5. Afterward, your officiant, yourselves, and any required witnesses must sign the license. (In some states, an officiant counts as a witness, but not in others.)

6. Then, your officiant returns the signed marriage license to the courthouse for filing.

7. Go party.

A few weeks after your marriage license is filed, you'll receive a marriage certificate in the mail— but only if you requested it, as most states won't send it automatically. Simply put, a marriage certificate is a public record stating that you are legally married and to whom; when and where it took place; and the name of the performing officiant. So, it's imperative to request a copy of the marriage certificate as this is the document you'll need to show in order to legally change your last name, add your spouse to your employment benefits, or avoid any issues should you get audited by the IRS.

Also, it's a good idea to request multiple copies of your marriage certificate. This will cost a few extra bucks but is totally worth it should your home get broken into or destroyed by a natural disaster. Put one in a safe at home, another in a safe-deposit box, and another with a highly trusted relative or friend.

What's up with the blood test? Before the rubella vaccine was developed in 1969, the disease was widespread and often deadly among newborns, so people were required to submit a blood test for it prior to marriage. Thanks to widespread vaccination, rubella was eliminated from the United States by 2004, making a blood test unnecessary, and in 2019, Montana became the last state to phase it out.

WHEN YOUR LOVE CAN'T WAIT

These thirty-two states, plus Washington, DC, have no waiting period, meaning you can apply for a marriage license and get married on the same day.

Alabama	Maine	Ohio
Arizona	Minnesota	Oklahoma
Arkansas	Mississippi	Rhode Island
California	Missouri	South Dakota
Colorado	Montana	Tennessee
Connecticut	Nebraska	Utah
Georgia	Nevada	Vermont
Hawaii	New Hampshire	Virginia
Idaho	New Mexico	Washington, DC
Indiana	North Carolina	West Virginia
Kentucky	North Dakota	Wyoming

Where You Can Marry Yourselves

Colorado

To solemnize, or perform, your own marriage in Colorado, simply head to a county clerk's office with a photo ID, apply for the marriage license, go marry yourselves, sign the license, and return it for filing. There's no witness requirement and no waiting period. Easy peasy.

Pennsylvania

In Pennsylvania, self-uniting marriages are known as Quaker weddings, which are rooted in the Quaker tradition of keeping things low-key and, well, traditional. First, apply for the standard marriage license and pay an additional fee for a Quaker license (also called a self-uniting license). Once you've secured both licenses, grab two witnesses and hold your ceremony wherever the heck you'd like. Afterward, all present parties must sign the certificate, which then gets returned to the courthouse for filing.

Washington, DC

Self-uniting marriages became legal in DC in 2014. Simply submit an application online, head to the marriage bureau at the H. Carl Moultrie Courthouse to show proper ID and pay the fee, leave the courthouse premises to marry yourselves, and return for the clerk's signature to make things official.

Note: California, Illinois, Kansas, Maine, Nevada, and Wisconsin are commonly listed on wedding websites as states that also allow self-solemnizing marriages, but there's some serious fine print here: They all require couples to declare their religious affiliation, denomination, or sect, and many require evidence to prove this.

> When looking into a state or county's marriage laws, be sure to visit the official website ending in ".gov" for the most up-to-date information, as it changes often.

Guest or No Guests

Because today's elopements come in many forms, not just the book-it-to-Mexico variety, some affairs include a handful of guests. How many guests is up to you to decide, but keep in mind that it might actually be *harder* to pare down an elopement guest list than create one for a blowout wedding, so don't put it off. To ensure it feels intimate, a good rule of thumb is no more than thirty to thirty-five guests. Beyond that, it starts to feel more like the kind of wedding you wished to avoid to begin with.

If you're having trouble deciding whom to invite, and your setting is a venue, it'll often make the call for you. Venues that reserve rooms for small wedding celebrations usually have tiers of pricing based on the number of guests present. For the majority of these, anything deemed "intimate" tops out at twenty-five to thirty guests. Other venues are intentionally intimate, established in buildings *because* of their small capacity limits set by the fire code.

For guidance on the guest list for an intimate ceremony, think about whom you'd have in your imaginary wedding party; chances are, these are the friends and family you'll want to have at your side when going small. By including them as guests at your intimate celebration instead of a bridal party in a traditional wedding, you'll endure zero passive-aggressive comments about

how broke they are because the bachelorette party cost this and the bridesmaid's dress they'll never wear again cost that.

If you're still having trouble win-nowing down the guest list, think about those who will be in your lives for the long run, for the pro-motions and babies and job losses and heartaches. Whom do you text first when something major—good or bad—happens? Invite them.

Budget and Finances

Given the $30,000+ price tag of the average wedding these days, eloping is an incredible way to set you up for a strong financial future together. But even though you're saving major cash, you still have to spend some coin, so get on the same page here, and quickly. Do you want to tap into savings and splurge on a destination elope-ment? Or keep it lean and opt for a backyard barbecue? Maybe you fall somewhere in between and go for a local gallery that specializes in intimate ceremonies or throw a private dinner party at your favorite restaurant. Whatever you choose, make sure your spending deci-sions and amounts align before you start firming things up.

MARRIAGE AND TAXES

What happens when a tax accountant and a consulting actuary get engaged? While five months pregnant? They head straight to a tax advisor to figure out how to file.

Dee (the tax accountant) and Dave (the consulting actuary) met on Tinder in late 2015. After their first date, they were inseparable for eight days, and dated for just over five months before getting engaged. Along the way she got pregnant, and after having the baby, they decided in early December to visit a tax advisor to determine how to file their taxes the following spring. He advised that the best decision was for them to get married by the end of the year, as filing status depends on marital status as of December 31. If they got married in time, they'd be able to file jointly, which would be the most advantageous option for them.

Dee immediately secured the private second floor of a Tuscan-Italian restaurant in their Pittsburgh neighborhood. She did her own hair and makeup and baked the wedding cake. Her single splurges were her wedding dress and veil from David's Bridal (which cost $2,500, "more than the wedding itself, LOL"). On December 30, 2016, in front of a festively decorated fireplace and surrounded by fifteen loved ones, they were legally married by a senior district judge who was also a family friend. The next day, New Year's Eve, they took off with their baby to Ft. Lauderdale for their honeymoon. They're planning to have a big party for their ten-year wedding anniversary.

And however fiscally savvy both may be, Dave still splurged on the engagement ring: a two-carat princess-cut diamond with diamond chips in the band.

Financial Past

One of the best things you can do before eloping is to meet with a financial advisor. It's probably not going to be fun, but you owe it to yourself and your partner to be honest about any debt, secret bank accounts, and salaries. And don't do what the majority of couples do and wait until the last minute—give yourselves a few months to work through any issues that might arise.

Prenups

A prenup, or prenuptial agreement—while not the most romantic of topics—is one of the first things a couple should discuss after getting engaged (if you're hesitant, call up a friend or family member who's gone through a divorce for some real talk). At its most basic, a prenup is an agreement between two people before they get married that changes what would be required under normal state law for a divorce. Basically, you're amending your state's divorce laws based on your individual financial situations.

If you decide to get a prenup, don't settle for the boilerplate one an attorney might hand you. It's not

nearly as simple as, "What's mine is mine and what's yours is yours." One of you might be set to inherit a windfall of money or be poised for a big promotion within the next year. Be sure to carve out what will happen to your future money before signing a prenup.

Also useful to know is what happens to the money that you earned and the belongings that you owned *before* signing that really important document, the marriage license. For instance, if one person has her own retirement account, her own separate bank account, and her own car, that's technically separate property that stays hers after she marries—it's never mixed with her spouse's money. It doesn't matter when they started dating, when they got engaged, or when they married—whatever wealth and property she acquired up to the second she signs the marriage license is *her separate property* for the entire marriage.

However, anything she contributes to her retirement account the moment *after* she signs the marriage license is considered marital, or joint, property. From this point on, she's sharing her retirement, including her own contributions, her employer's, and any market growth—but only what is put in after marriage. So if she had

$25,000 in her retirement account before getting married, that's still her own money in the instance of divorce; if a divorce happens, any gains to that $25,000 after signing the marriage license get divided— *unless there is a prenup stating otherwise that's already in place*.

It's not a jazzy topic, but given that lack of communication about money is a leading cause of divorce, it's one that should be approached honestly and openly, without judgment.

What the heck is a postnup? It works the same as a prenup, except a couple gets one after they're already married. This often happens when a couple doesn't understand their individual assets before tying the knot.

Student Loan Debt

A big misconception about entering into marriage with student loan debt is that once you're married, the debt is now the other person's responsibility too. That's simply not the case. Here's what really happens: When you already have student loan debt going into the marriage, it's considered separate debt. It's not your spouse's problem unless he attaches himself as a cosigner. That's it.

What *can* cause a sticky financial situation, however, is how you file your taxes. Depending on which student loan repayment plan you're on, if you file your taxes jointly, this merged income will now be used to determine your new monthly payment. The higher your income looks to the student loan folks based on what the IRS has on file, the higher your monthly payment will be. This is only applicable if you're on a repayment plan that's driven by your income.

However, there's no requirement to *ever* file jointly, so you don't need to wait until your loans are paid off or forgiven before getting married. When doing your taxes, select the married-filing-separately option; while it's the least advantageous in terms of the amount of tax return dollars you'll receive from the government, your monthly loan payment will still be based on just *your* income.

Bottom line: Some couples will benefit by filing their taxes jointly, and some simply won't. It's best to talk to an accountant before making this call (or getting married).

Vows

The most common thing couples forget to do when eloping is write their vows. Or, since many people are reluctant writers, they avoid them until they're mid-flight, or it's the morning-of. Vows are far more meaningful (and *far* less stressful) if they spill out over time, even if they start as snippets in a "Why I Love You" note in your phone that you drafted on the elliptical at the gym.

And remember, by eloping, you eliminate public speaking in front of a large audience. Saying your vows becomes a truly intimate moment to be shared by the two of you and any guests you feel comfortable inviting—whether that's zero or twenty.

> Back in the day, couples used to write love letters to each other the night before they got married, place them in a box, and read them on their first anniversary.

Registry

There's a solid chance that if you're already living together as a couple, you're good on bath towels and sheets, and will only use that immersion blender once before relegating it to the back of the cupboard (or Goodwill). Skip the hassle of creating a traditional registry, and instead, if your loved ones are adamant about giving you a gift, suggest that they contribute to something you've been saving for as a couple, such as a new car, bathroom renovation, or honeymoon.

If this sounds like an awkward conversation to have, registry website Zola has got you covered. The site allows you to essentially register for money with its "cash fund" option, presented as a variety of gifts and experiences. Your loved ones simply select from a menu of cash fund "gifts," including things as far-ranging as a $300 couples massage or a $10,000 down payment on a house (one can dream). Then, the money that was used to purchase these "gifts" gets transferred to your bank account and voilà, you receive money without actually asking for money.

Receiving gifts is nice, but why do couples create registries to tell their guests what they want? Back in the 1920s, traditional wedding gifts included silver, china, linen, and crystal. To avoid duplicates, the department store Marshall Field's invented the wedding registry to show what's already been purchased.

Pickup or delivery? If your love language includes "extra cheese" and "delivery," you're set: Domino's has a wedding registry. Essentially, you "register" for a bevy of classed-up pizza deals, such as "The Wedding Night," "Post-Honeymoon Adjustment to Real Life," and "Thank You Card-a-thon," which are delivered as eGift cards and range in value from $15 to $100.

Air Horn: The Announcement

Breaking the news that you eloped will inevitably have to happen, whether it's before or after your elopement, so give some thought as to how you wish to go about it. Before you turn to social media to announce it, think about how family members and close friends who are out of the loop might react. A thoughtful paper announcement with a handwritten signature and personal sentiment goes far. When sitting down to draft and order your announcements, be sure to include the date of your actual elopement (what you consider your anniversary).

Here's a good strategy for how to deliver the news:

- Parents: Tell them in person or by phone before the elopement or immediately after.

- Immediate and close family members: Mail a paper announcement after the elopement and call those you're particularly close to. Many paper companies that cater to large weddings now have a line for elopements.

- Close friends: Mail a paper announcement after the elopement and call your closest friends.

- Distant family and friends: Mail a paper announcement after the elopement.

- Colleagues and acquaintances: Email an announcement or let them find out on social media.

CHAPTER 2:

Vendors

Haylie & Kevin

After returning from a trip to Mexico to scout vendors for her two-hundred-person wedding, Haylie, a florist, was just about to sign her venue contract when she realized she just couldn't go through with it. "I had a pit in my stomach," she says. "I'm a floral and event designer. I knew how I wanted it to look, and I know what that [costs]—it's a $500,000 wedding."

Cost aside, Haylie says she also felt that a big wedding just didn't fit who she and her fiancé, Kevin, really are—they don't take themselves too seriously and are pretty laid-back. When she brought up ditching it, he immediately agreed. "We both felt relieved for the first time in a while—which happens when you finally align your feelings to your plans," she says.

The decision to toss the traditional wedding was smooth. "The rocky part was figuring out what we wanted to do instead," says Haylie. They knew they still wanted to get married in Mexico, since that's where Kevin first said "I love you." But now, halfway to their wedding date, they had to find a new venue, determine whom to invite, and decide on how to celebrate after the wedding. "Ultimately, finding the cliff-top villa was what made everything click for us."

The villa—a ten-bedroom luxury estate in Cabo San Lucas that overlooks the Pacific Ocean—dictated their remaining decisions, starting with the guest list. Haylie and Kevin pared it down to thirty-five, prioritizing their immediate family members and those who would have been bridesmaids or groomsmen, along with their significant others. The villa also served as a multipurpose venue, hosting a welcome party on the beach; the wedding ceremony, which was held on the pool deck that overlooks Cabo's white sand beaches; a cocktail hour; and the plated dinner afterward.

Given her industry experience, Haylie knew exactly which vendors to prioritize—and who to call. She first hired an event coordinator she's known for years, and then selected a photographer and videographer she'd worked with on past weddings and photo-shoots. For florals, her coordinator pointed her to a local florist, Lola del Campo of Florenta Flower Design, with whom Haylie worked very closely Io design bouton-nières for the fathers and brothers, the ceremony floral backdrop, the reception florals for the tables, and the backdrop for the sweet-heart table.

As for the bouquet? Like a true pro, Haylie made her own—the morn-ing of the wedding. It was a mix of dried florals and grasses with hellebores, sweet peas, ranuncu-lus, and garden roses, which are some of her favorite blooms.

On being a florist and working with one on such a momentous occasion, Haylie says, "It was great. Lola is such an artist that I really trusted her, and she truly went above and beyond. She took everything in my head and made it reality. She nailed it."

From a wedding-vendor-turned-bride perspective, Haylie says, "I feel like I have a deeper under-standing of the pressures and expectations my couples are fac-ing from their peers, their family, and themselves, and it will be that much easier to help them now.

"Ultimately, eloping and having an intimate wedding felt right because we got to let go of the expectations of others and really create something that felt like 'us' that our closest family and friends would remember."

The only thing she'd do differ-ently? "Make the decision sooner to elope and have an intimate wedding."

Haylie & Kevin's Fine Print

LIVE: Washington, DC

WORK: Haylie is a floral and event designer, and Kevin is a senior sales associate at a commercial lending company.

AGES WHEN THEY ELOPED: Both were twenty-eight.

KEVIN'S FIRST IMPRESSION: "She wasn't what I expected."

HAYLIE'S FIRST IMPRESSION: "He wasn't what I expected."

RELATIONSHIP TIME LINE: Dated for six years → Engaged for ten months → Eloped February 2020 → Mini-mooned at the villa for five days following their ceremony

WEDDING VENUE: Villa La Roca

DISTANCE FROM HOME TO VENUE: 2,912 miles / 4,686 km

NUMBER OF GUESTS: 35

HE WORE: A dark brown custom suit from Alton Lane

SHE WORE: The Giovanna gown from Sarah Seven

RINGS: They designed Haylie's engagement ring together. Their wedding bands are from Holden Rings.

REGISTRY: They included a registry page on their wedding website. It says, "We have lived together for three years . . . we don't need spoons. Just come to Cabo and give us the adult spring break we have been asking for. Thanks!"

SPENT: $180,000 (Haylie and Kevin covered the four-day vacation-slash-weekend for their family and friends, so much of this figure comes from the $5,500/night villa, the welcome party, and a boat excursion the day following the ceremony.)

A Whole New Vendor World

As modern wedding venues have evolved from the church basement to the hotel ballroom to a plethora of intimate, personal options, so too have vendors. Many vendors began their careers doing traditional weddings before expanding into smaller, simpler affairs. The amazing travel opportunities are one obvious draw for them to make this shift, but a lesser-discussed reason is the need to reduce their *own* stress due to high-strung moms and that one drunk uncle who is impossible to wrangle for the group shot, Saturday after Saturday after Saturday.

Stress is likely how you arrived here too. Whether you've decided on a quick courthouse ceremony followed by a mellow bistro lunch with a handful of loved ones or barefoot vows on the breezy, carved-out beaches of Oahu, chances are you'll still want to track down a vendor (or four) ahead of time. Perhaps you're splurging on flowers, and your vision for an intimate, at-home dinner party includes a table runner made of lamb's ear studded with toffee roses, something beyond the scope of what Trader Joe's can offer. And speaking of dinner, you're going to want to celebrate with great food and drinks, whether it's just the two of you or a guest count of twenty. Above all, you definitely, *definitely* want great photographs.

Here are some key vendors to consider hiring as you plot your chill day.

Photographer

Whether your elopement is just you and yours, sans guests, or a handful of your closest loved ones, one of the only ways to share the experience with everyone *else* is with photos, the lasting takeaway from the day. For that reason, selecting a photographer will be one of the most important decisions you make in the planning process. Find someone with experience and set an interview ASAP—most also do big, traditional weddings and tend to book a year out.

First and Foremost: You Need to Really Like This Person

If nothing else, splurge on a great photographer. He or she will be spending many, often intense, hours with you, without the wall of protection provided by a wedding party or three hundred guests. Not only that, but he or she will also be one of the few witnesses to one of the most intimate and important days of your life. If you elope in a state that requires witnesses, your photographer (and assistant, if there is one) can step in and sign the marriage license.

Finding Your Photographer

There is a raft of talented wedding photographers who've expanded their menu of options to include elopements. Just know that many have ditched traditional, big-box listings and simply use social media and their own websites for referrals. Find photographers who specialize in elopements and intimate weddings via a quick Google search of the term "elopement photographer," followed by the destination you're interested in. This will produce a list of photographers who live in the area or have experience shooting there.

Next, spend a decent amount of time on the websites of photographers whose galleries showcase the look and feel you're going for: moody and dramatic, playful and airy, crisp and cinematic. Some shoot digital as well as film. If your elopement involves travel abroad, you're going to want a photographer whose portfolio highlights expertise in the country or city where you're headed (even better if she or he speaks the language).

Above all, keep in mind that you're going to want someone who's actually photographed an elopement before (experience that applies to every other vendor you decide to hire as well). Any kind of travel or

THE INSTAGRAM RABBIT HOLE

If you've got five hours to kill, go ahead and plug in some hashtags on Instagram and see what turns up—you will absolutely find millions of options for #elopementphotographerPLACEYOUAREELOPINGTO. Just know that Instagram, for all its virtues in connecting us globally, has plenty of faults, not the least of which is that it's not a search engine; you can't just churn out a sea of hashtagged posts that can then be searched through using keywords. Plus, the person you think is your dream photographer might just be a travel blogger who wants to grow his brand by hashtagging every trendy thing he doesn't actually do—starting with #elopementphotography. Save yourself a dozen DMs down the path to nowhere and just start with Google (this applies to all of your other vendors as well).

trekking can involve hiccups and stress—without the added element of getting married—so it's crucial that your photographer is experienced enough to know the basics, such as the need for packing a backup camera and lenses in a carry-on bag should his or her luggage get lost.

When to Hire Your Photographer

If your elopement isn't a huge rush, aim to hire your photographer a year out, because, as previously mentioned, most also do traditional weddings, and this is the time frame they use for *all* bookings. If you find your dream photographer, but she's not free on the date you originally chose, be prepared to be flexible (often photographers have more flexibility midweek than weekends). It all depends on the photographer's personal situation (kids or no kids, propensity for last-minute travel, having a full-time job) and workload. Once you've found your dream candidate and lined up dates, you'll do an interview, either in person, over the phone, or as a video call.

If you don't have a firm date but want to lock in a photographer, a safe bet is to offer a loose set of dates that fall midweek, which creates a time frame that a photographer is more likely to work with until you settle on one. Just be considerate, particularly during wedding season—which now not only includes spring and summer, but fall too—and don't reach out to hire a photographer without a date in mind. While being a chill couple makes it a pleasant experience for all parties, don't let your planning get *too* lax. Without an official date, a photographer can't arrange for travel, and it's fairly well documented that flights don't get cheaper the closer things get to takeoff, so once you have your date, stick to it.

TRADITIONS TO KEEP

While so much about eloping involves tossing tradition aside, there are some elements that you might want to keep when it comes to the photos. Here, Florida-based photographer Joshua Kane Wood shares which traditions to consider keeping.

Engagement Session

Prior to a nontraditional wedding, Wood offers couples engagement sessions. "Nobody likes being photographed, and it's a way to warm up," he says. Engagement shoots also give couples the chance to capture photos in another place, or another season, than their elopement date. Plus, they enhance the relationship between the couple and the photographer. "By the time the elopement rolls around, I've already got such good rapport with the couple," he says.

First Look

Another tradition to consider keeping is the first look, which lends itself well to intimate ceremonies. Historically, a first look refers to the moment when a bride or groom looks down the aisle and sees his or her fiancé(e) for the first time that day. It's an extremely emotionally charged event, not just for the couple, but also for the guests who witness it. In recent years, the term as it pertains to elopements has evolved to mean a first look between a couple in a setting of their choice—usually there is no "aisle" (or audience, for that matter). Wood aims to intentionally separate the couple, first shooting solitary portraits of whoever requires the least amount of time to get ready while the other person finishes up. From his experience capturing these first looks, after they see each other, most couples immediately hug and kiss. "Inevitably, they'll laugh. Without fail."

Shot List

For an intimate ceremony with family and a few friends, provide your photographer with a short shot list so they have a heads-up as to which moments and groupings are important to you. The style will vary depending on your photographer, of course, but plan to allot five minutes per shot. Some ideas might include one partner waiting for the other during the first look, candid getting-ready shots, close-ups of your faces during your vows, the untouched tablescape before your celebratory meal, and, of course, the kiss.

If the elopement is a secret, be sure to let your photographer know not to post anything on her social media platforms until you've made your own announcement, should a family member or friend follow her and see your news on her Instagram feed first. Not an ideal way to break the news.

What do photographers wish you knew before booking them? Alex Mari, an elopement photographer whose experience spans both coasts, shares her two cents: "I don't care how majestic that waterfall is or how mind-blowing the mountains are, if you as a couple are feeling uncomfortable because you push yourself to make the day fit the mold you see with all of the Instagram elopements, you're not going to love the photos."

Money and Contracts

Ah, the conversation no one wants to have, so let's have it within the gentle confines of this book. When you hire a photographer (and most other vendors), a contract will quickly hit your inbox, which usually accompanies an invoice for a nonrefundable deposit, typically 30 to 50 percent of the total rate. If travel is involved, you'll likely receive a separate invoice—up front—with the payment terms outlined, which sometimes surprises couples.

For vendors, this is the same rodeo as if they were booking a big wedding. "If a couple hires a photographer to document their wedding or elopement in a different city or state (or even country), a travel fee is typically added to the package," says photographer Lauren Miller of Lauren Louise Collective in Washington, DC. "Just because a couple is eloping doesn't mean they'll necessarily save on photography expenses, especially if the celebration is abroad."

Miller's travel fee for an out-of-state wedding includes roundtrip airfare from DC; at minimum, a two-night hotel stay (she arrives at least a day early to allow for travel mishaps and to scope out the location); transportation to and from the airport and venue; and a per diem for food.

To prevent future awkward emails or, at worst, being dropped by a vendor for neglecting to pay on time (and rightfully so), see a preview of what to expect on pages 52–53. The first sample invoice (page 52) breaks down the costs for standard elopement photography rates plus travel, courtesy of Miller. This is for a five-hour elopement without a reception or second shooter.

For comparison, the invoice from Asheville-based Taylor Parker Photography (page 53) reflects an eight-hour elopement with two shooters, followed by an intimate reception.

Note that photographers' rates aren't just dictated by their expertise, but also where they live and how competitive the market is (metropolitan areas will cost more than rural).

And remember, because there is no one way to elope, sometimes the money rules do get tossed. Photographers looking to add a new aesthetic to their portfolios might cut a deal in exchange for greater creative control. Bonus: More photos for you.

Day-of Time Line

After the date is settled and the photographer is booked, the next thing to tackle is how to map out the day. For most photographers who capture outdoor weddings, the ideal time to shoot is at sunset or sunrise, when the lighting is softest. However, sunrise shoots aren't always worth the early wake-up call that's required to get everything (and everyone) organized. If your photographer is fond of capturing early-morning tones,

and you're game, just be sure to set an alarm. For 3 a.m.

An experienced photographer will research the time of sunrise and sunset at your location and create a day-of time line that either moves forward from the sunrise shoot, or backward from sunset. Two to three hours before the ceremony, most photographers shoot the "getting ready" slot of time, those quiet moments when the cuff links rest on a windowsill, the rings sit waiting in a crystal dish on the dresser, the dress hangs in a window. This also provides a chance to review the time line for the rest of the day and make any adjustments if inclement weather rolls in.

If your elopement takes place in a particularly extreme environment, requiring your photographer to (literally) go to great lengths to secure amazing shots for you, be gracious and tip *generously*.

Lauren Louise Collective

ELOPEMENT PHOTOGRAPHY PACKAGE*

ELOPEMENT PHOTOGRAPHY PACKAGE   + $5,000.00

ONE PHOTOGRAPHER (LAUREN LOUISE)

5 HOURS OF PHOTOGRAPHY COVERAGE

300+ EDITED, HIGH RESOLUTION FILES

ONLINE GALLERY + USB

PERSONAL PRINTING RIGHTS

+ TAXABLE

SUBTOTAL: $5,000.00

6% DC SALES TAX: $300.00

TOTAL: $5,300.00

Taylor Parker

PHOTOGRAPHY*

DESCRIPTION

8 HOUR ELOPEMENT + RECEPTION COVERAGE

2 PHOTOGRAPHERS

DIGITAL IMAGES + PRINT RIGHTS

12 X 12 CRAFTED WEDDING ALBUM

100 FINE ART PRINTS

TOTAL AMOUNT: $5,200.00

NC TAX: 4.75%

AMOUNT DUE: $5,447.00

---

*Rates as of 2021

What the heck is "blue hour"? You've likely heard of golden hour, that slice of time aligning with breakfast and happy hour when everyone's skin looks airbrushed. Blue hour hits twice a day: just before the sun comes out, when the slowly lightening sky lends a blue-colored tint to the landscape, and right after sunset, when the horizon has just swallowed the sun, again giving a cool blue glow to the surroundings. Elopement photographers often seek out this time of day, as the moody blue tones lend themselves to conveying emotions and serenity.

Videographer

Documenting your elopement with videography creates a powerful cinematic experience, one you can watch on anniversaries for years to come. Olivia Graziano, a videographer based in Syracuse, New York, considers the medium another great way to share your elopement experience with loved ones. For instance, one couple she filmed held a backyard barbecue a few months after they eloped and played their video for their guests.

Graziano says a perk of filming elopements and small weddings is the richness and diversity of audio that can be captured and incorporated due to the sheer intimacy of it all—birds chirping, waves crashing, a crackling campfire. You want an experienced videographer who has a solid portfolio of destination wedding or elopement work; a red flag is a video collection with no audio. Most videographers overlay the footage with music, and Graziano sends couples a questionnaire in advance to determine what style of music feels like them (elegant, upbeat, classic) and then tries to match a song to their style. The finished film often includes interspersed snippets of the couple reciting their vows, which can be quite powerful when hearing them while at the same time watching the finished video.

And because elopements tend to be much more laid-back than big weddings, a videographer has a generous amount of time to set up and capture more technical shots. For these instances, Graziano uses a drone to capture aerial views. If you wish to hire a videographer who uses drones, be sure to check the rules and regulations for your ceremony location as they vary by city, state, and country.

> Elopement videographers usually charge as much for elopements as they do for traditional weddings. While the price tag ranges widely depending on your elopement's location and the videographer's level of experience, the average cost in the US is around $2,000, but can range from $1,000 to $5,000 and up, depending on the package you select.

Officiants

While the photographer is the star of the vendor show, the officiant is, more often than not, left for the third act. You're so close to riding off into your metaphorical sunset that you forget to tie up the loose end of hiring the one person who will actually make any of this *legal*.

The technical talk here is important: It's become incredibly common for couples who elope to ask a loved one to marry them, leading to quickie online ordinations and, unfortunately, overlooked steps. If you decide to go with an officiant you aren't familiar with, make sure he or she is authorized through a legitimate organization for the area you're marrying in. If you have doubts, double-check with the courthouse to be sure he or she is valid.

> Looking to get ordained in less than a minute, for free? American Marriage Ministries is a nondenominational, nonreligious online ordination service founded in 2009 on the basis that every couple has the constitutionally protected right to enter into the institution of marriage on their own terms, which includes the right to choose who performs their wedding ceremony.
>
> If you're not religious, don't get tripped up by the word "minister" as you research officiants. The term doesn't always denote religious affiliation and is now often used interchangeably with "officiant." Both individuals are authorized to do the same thing—legally validate your marriage license.

Paying Your Officiant

This is one of the trickier areas when it comes to paying vendors. If you're hiring a minister, but your ceremony is outside their place of worship, and therefore you're not paying to use the space, a donation is a generous (and common) gesture. Some officiants use a contract, but this widely varies, so check the fine print regarding a deposit, cancellation policy (sometimes traffic happens and officiants miss the whole thing), and who is covering the cost of the marriage license and subsequent copies.

On the other hand, if the officiant is a relative, friend, or loved one, whether it's your uncle who's a pastor or your BFF who got ordained, you can probably plan *not* to pay him or her. Instead, a gift is a nice way to say thank you. And, as with your other vendors, if you're heading out of town, assume you're covering travel, lodging, and meals for your officiant—even if this is your best friend since second grade, you're still taking her away from her regular daily life of doing whatever she does to pay rent.

Florist

Ever wonder why wedding florals are an $8 billion industry? Probably not, but incorporating flowers into weddings has ancient roots, tracing back to when Greek brides carried garlands or donned floral crowns to signify good fortune (we think they were probably inspired by the 776 BC Olympic Games).

Today, many brides carry bouquets (and wear floral crowns) and likely always will because, well, they're gorgeous, and what else are you going to do with your hands? As modern weddings have invited flowers and greenery into every aspect of the affair—boutonnières, corsages, centerpieces, wreaths, garlands, arches, walls, dog crowns, dangling chandeliers made of upside-down tulips—florists have shifted toward accommodating smaller affairs as well. Burlap-loving Farmgirl Flowers in San Francisco offers a City Hall Collection in a "romantic palette" of whites and soft corals, which can be overnighted anywhere in the continental United States.

Of course, any bouquet is an elopement bouquet if you call it that. If you're using a florist near the location of your ceremony, find out ahead of time whether they deliver, so you can plan accordingly. Store flowers in a cool, dark room or refrigerator so they last longer. Or, if you want the blooms to open up overnight, put them somewhere warm.

And, because every season is elopement season, here are some flower varieties you can typically expect to find at any US florist shop, year-round, plus what they signify:

- Baby's breath: Everlasting love
- Calla lilies: Beauty
- Freesia: Trust and innocence
- Gardenias: Purity
- Gerbera daisies: Happiness
- Hydrangeas: Heartfelt emotion
- Orchids: Beauty and fertility
- Snapdragons: Graciousness

Really want some flora and fauna ambience without dropping thousands of bucks on installations? Get married in late November or early December at a quaint venue that will be festively decorated, such as a bed-and-breakfast or a mountain lodge.

If you'd like to sustainably get rid of your flowers, check to see whether a local farm will take them—as long as they aren't sprayed with pesticides.

Hair and Makeup

There aren't many times in life that call for having your hair professionally styled or your makeup expertly done, so, if you're so inclined, you should absolutely treat yourself the day you get married.

Hair Stylist

As soon as you find a hair stylist whose style you like, hit up that contact form, as stylists book up just as quickly (and as far out) as other vendors. He or she might include a trial in the pricing model, which you should absolutely take advantage of, as this is the best way to test your hairstyle and steer your stylist in the right direction as far as which products to use.

When choosing your do for the big day, consider the environment in which you're eloping—coastal and windy, tropical and humid, mountainous and arid—and talk to your stylist for tips.

Makeup Stylist

If you're treating yourself to professional makeup, here's what to do to make things run as smoothly as possible.

1. Share the specific venue well in advance so your stylist can get a sense of how much natural light there is to work with.

2. Create a day-of time line and agree on a firm start time.

3. Get your hair done before your makeup. This is very, very important.

4. Ask your makeup artist to hang out, post-ceremony, to touch up makeup before the photos (hi, tears). It might cost more, but it's worth it. If he or she needs to bolt, pack a DIY touch-up kit with these ten items: mascara, eye liner, eyeshadow, primer, concealer, foundation, bronzer, blush, lipstick, and lip liner.

The Dress

Classic. Boho. Understated. Whatever your vibe, embrace it—there is no singular "elopement look." We've interviewed hundreds of couples and seen just as much tulle on a cliff as we have silk in a pristine garden. But if you're overwhelmed by the ocean of white lace out there, here are some tips to guide your search for The Dress, based on your taste and aesthetic.

Classic

Do you perk up at the mention of "ball gown" or "satin A-line?" Look for timeless silhouettes and embellishments—think sweetheart necklines, scalloped trains, tulle skirts, button closures, and anything that references Grace Kelly.

Boho

While the boho wedding dress is here to stay, it's certainly evolved from the Coachella-inspired, fringe-forward styles of the early 2010s to something a bit more high-fashion. Think: off-the-shoulder split sleeves, lush trains with crochet overlay, and elegant empire waists that invoke the free spiritedness once singularly captured by a gorgeous flower crown (but, to be honest, we're still here for those).

Eco-conscious

If the environment is a top priority when selecting a dress, look for something vintage (here's a great opportunity to make this your "something borrowed"). Or look for a dress made from reused material, such as restored lace, which is often sourced from Europe—specifically, Parisian street markets—and lends a unique story to your gown.

Money-Saver

There are a handful of online retailers that offer pre-owned dresses or the option of buying a sample sale dress (see Resources on page 219). But the biggest piece of advice if you're looking to save money? Shop for dresses any-where but bridal and wedding out-lets. The same satin slip dress on a wedding dress site will cost much more than a similar one from a standard retailer.

The Wedding Suit

Why not take this opportunity to invest in a tailored suit? We love a crème fitted suit, a look that's elevated to wedding-day-worthy when worn with a lace camisole or satin crop top. Or wear what the French call *le smoking*—a wom-an's tuxedo, a striking display of confidence and empowerment.

Pulling Double Duty

If your goal is to be chic as well as practical, invest in an outfit you'll wear again. Your elopement jumpsuit can easily transform into the attire you rock at a future office party, or someone else's wedding.

If you're eloping outdoors, *really* think about footwear. Hiking in heels is, shall we say, *difficult*, so pack boots or sneakers, and give any guests a heads-up here too.

The Rings

Nowadays, it's fairly common to get engaged without a ring. Women are often financially independent before marriage and want to help pay for the ring, lead-ing to more ring-less proposals and joint trips to the jeweler. This creates something of a "ring journey," a bonding experience as you go through the design process together. (Also, it's the twenty-first century, and by now, both sexes should have ditched the antiquated idea that rings signify ownership.)

Or propose to one another. Enter-ing into an engagement with a double proposal—which is when both partners propose on the same day or different ones—means no one has the upper hand over the other, as can be implied with traditional proposals where one person asks and the other

JUST PIN IT

Ashley Peters, a.k.a. The Stylist Abroad, began doing elopements globally in 2018 and has since done hair for brides in Iceland, Croatia, Italy, and the Netherlands. Here's what she keeps in her bag to create hair magic, wherever she is:

Curling iron	Brush	Shine spray
Cordless curling iron	Converters for European outlets	Wax stick
Hair wand	Strong-hold hairspray	Anti-frizz products
Teasing comb	Texture spray	Extension cord

She'd also like you to know that around 70 percent of photos on Pinterest use extensions, so be open to using—and paying for—them if you want to transform your medium-length bob into a boho-chic, half-up fishtail with a braided crown.

responds. Instead, the engagement begins with a sense of unity, equality, and a strong signal to each other that you'll be there for the long haul, romantically *and* emotionally.

Many couples have also said goodbye to the traditional diamond engagement ring. Reasons for this vary, ranging from the ethical standards in which diamonds are mined to the strain they put on the environment to simply wanting a ring with deeper personal meaning or family history.

Whatever you do, don't go into debt for your ring. Here are some money-saving tips to keep in mind as you launch your ring journey together: Look for rose gold or silver bands, which are more affordable than platinum or gold. Avoid white gold, as it's brittle, meaning the stone can pop off more easily.

If you want to splurge on the rock, leave the setting plain, as it's easier to jazz up when you have more money to do so down the road.

If you or yours is set on a diamond ring, save money by hovering just below the point at which the price jumps based on carat weight, which is the half- or quarter-carat mark. And don't get hung up on clarity, which measures the flawlessness of a diamond—microscopic blemishes can't be seen with the naked eye.

> The "mengagement" ring is a thing. It's not as lame as it sounds—many boutique jewelers offer a set of two jeweled bands, one thicker for him and one thinner for her.

> During engagement season—between Thanksgiving and Valentine's Day—proposals surge, which means prices do too, so avoid buying a ring during this stretch of time.

Make Sure Your Diamond Lasts Forever

A diamond requires special care. Susie Saltzman, a New York City designer who cut her teeth at Tiffany & Co. before launching a specialized fine jewelry business, offers three pro tips for caring for yours:

1. Invest in a spacer band, a simple, cheaper, all-metal band worn between the wedding band and engagement ring. Since diamonds are the hardest substance on earth, they will inevitably scratch whatever they frequently come into contact with—your wedding band. This is particularly important if your wedding band contains diamonds, since diamonds can scratch—and chip—one another.

2. Avoid having your diamond cleaned with the latest ultrasonic device, as the ultrasound waves that clean your diamond can also loosen it. Instead, head to the kitchen sink. Plug it. Place your ring in a bowl with warm water and dish soap (any mild soap will do), and let it soak for twenty minutes. Diamonds attract oil from our hands and lotion, making them cloudy, so the

chemical reaction that lifts grease and oil from dirty dishes has the same effect on diamonds. Then, gently brush the ring with an old, soft toothbrush and rinse it under warm water. Dry it with a soft cotton cloth, or let it air-dry.

3. Put your ring in the same safe place every time you take it off. Designate a spot in your jewelry box to avoid the panic that typically comes when you take it off to go to the gym or clean your apartment and set it in a different place every time. Also, in order to avoid scratching, make sure none of your rings in said designated space are touching each other.

A GEMSTONE IS ALSO FOREVER

We love the look of a jewel-toned rock where a diamond usually rests. Here are some gemstones to consider, along with what they symbolize.

Emerald: Abundance in success and riches

Opal: Playfulness and strength

Ruby: Purity and passion

Sapphire: Wisdom, loyalty, and faith

Tourmaline: Happiness and healing

WHAT'S AN ETHICALLY SOURCED RING?

To truly be considered ethical, a ring should meet the following four criteria:

1. **Traceable:** Your jeweler can trace the gemstone to where it was mined, which should be a conflict-free area.
2. **Fair Trade:** The gemstone's journey from the mine site to the jeweler didn't stop at any sweatshops along the way to being cut and polished, but rather was handled by those in local communities who are paid a livable wage.
3. **Recycled:** Here, the band is made of old gold or platinum that went through a refining process to be restored to its original condition.
4. **Manufacturing:** Make sure your jeweler doesn't rely on manufacturing from a country with poor working conditions and pay.

Additionally, some ethical jewelers only use mercury-free gold. Traditionally, gold is found inside rocks deep in the ground, and after they're dug up, the gold is separated from the rock using mercury, which also happens to be a major pollutant. A mercury-free jeweler uses gold that has been panned by local miners.

Lab-grown diamonds are a point of controversy in the jewelry industry. Advocates argue that because they are created in an environment that requires no mining, they're an ethical choice. Those opposed say that the ethics here are moot because the diamonds are still manufactured on equipment made in countries with poor working conditions. Whatever your stance, lab-grown diamonds have the same physical and chemical characteristics as a natural diamond and are often significantly cheaper.

the ring today but aren't proposing for two months, your name and your money are attached until you hear "Yes!" and slide that ring on. Then, it becomes the other person's obligation to be named on the policy, and it's probably good form to discuss how to pay for the policy *together* at this point.

Insure Your Bling

Do *not* forget to do this, particularly if your elopement involves travel of any sort. Jewelers Mutual Insurance Group is the most trusted company in the industry, and you can sign up online or at the store when purchasing a ring. Geico and Progressive also offer jewelry insurance policies.

Important to know: Whomever is in possession of the ring needs to be named on the policy, so if you buy

MAKE IT A PACKAGE DEAL

If your approach to eloping is truly laissez-faire, or the time line is incredibly rushed, you can opt for an elopement package, which is becoming an increasingly popular option offered by boutique hotels and private resorts around the globe.

Take Acacia and Evan: Having grown frustrated with the endless decisions over every tiny detail while planning their winery wedding—"The forks were what set me off," says Acacia—they stopped short of signing the contract and instead eloped to Big Sur, where they had gotten engaged. Evan found elopement packages at cliffside getaway Post Ranch Inn and booked the $3,600 weekend option, which included a photographer, the officiant (who worked with them on personalized vows), the marriage license, a floral arrangement, custom-etched flutes, and a bottle of Champagne, which Acacia and Evan drank at 10 a.m. ("We were on East Coast time!") before saying their vows atop the cliffs overlooking the Pacific Ocean. They left Big Sur to honeymoon in Carmel-by-the-Sea, Napa, and Sonoma. Overall, the entire experience "was the best vacation ever," says Acacia.

They didn't entirely exclude their families, however. Before they left for Big Sur, they sent out invitations for a "Happily Ever After" party when they returned, held at Acacia's dad's country club in Maryland (both sets of parents loved the idea of eloping, and Acacia's mom spent hours picking out the perfect stamps for the party invitations). They hosted the party about six weeks after the elopement so the photos would be ready and created a website as part of their (very small) Zola registry to formally announce to family members that they had wed.

Any regrets? "Not a single one."

In 1908, playboy/heir to the *Washington Post* Edward Beale McLean eloped with socialite/heiress to her dad's gold rush riches Evalyn Walsh. During a lengthy honeymoon overseas, they stopped in Paris and met a jeweler named Pierre Cartier, who showed them the most expensive diamond in the world at the time, the Hope Diamond, then worth $180,000. Evalyn wasn't happy with the setting, though, so Cartier had it reset with the diamond mounted as a headpiece on a three-tiered circlet of large white diamonds. He brought it to Washington, DC, to let her borrow it for a weekend, a tactic that led to her purchasing it. She was the last private owner of the 45.52-carat, dark blue stone. It now sits in the Smithsonian's Natural Gem Collection and is worth a cool $350 mil.

ELOPEMENT CHECKLIST

- Accommodations
- Announcements
- Date
- Destination
- Flowers
- Food and drink
- Guest list (if any)
- Hair stylist
- Makeup artist
- Marriage laws
- Officiant
- Outfits
- Photographer
- Travel arrangements
- Venue
- Videographer
- Vows

CHAPTER 3:

Pack You Passpor

r

Katelyn &
Carlos

Katelyn and Carlos's love story began in 2009 in an airport hangar at JFK. Both were students at Syracuse University—she a junior, he a freshman—and said quick hellos to each other as they waited to board their flights to Florence for a semester abroad.

Once in Florence, they met up with a group of students to explore the city by night. Both quiet people, Katelyn and Carlos found themselves trailing behind the group, chatting about their backgrounds and where they grew up. While she was from Syracuse and he was from New Haven, which are around 300 miles [483 km] from each other, both of their grandparents had lived in neighboring towns in Upstate New York. They discovered that when they visited their grandparents in the summer as kids, they had both played at the only playground around for miles.

As they walked along the Arno River, they both recalled playing a very specific playground game called "woodchip warfare"—so specific that they *had* to have met as kids a decade prior. Says Katelyn of that evening's walk, "We've been almost inseparable ever since."

Nine years later, on the anniversary of the day they "re-met" in Florence, they eloped to the Tuscan city. "We live a very quiet life, so it seemed only natural to have a very intimate ceremony. We never really even considered a traditional wedding," says Katelyn. "We agreed on eloping before we even announced our engagement."

Their families were incredibly supportive, and not all that surprised, knowing how private the couple is. "If anything, they were more surprised that we got engaged after eight years together."

Immediately after having a civil ceremony at the Los Angeles County Registrar-Recorder/County Clerk, they hopped a red-eye to Rome, spent the night, took a train to Florence, and checked into Hotel Torre di Bellosguardo, a thirteenth-century villa-turned-hotel.

The next day, they held their symbolic ceremony in Boboli Gardens, in front of a fountain just off the Viottolone, a boulevard flanked by cypress trees. It was one of the places Katelyn loved most when she had studied abroad. Having left much of their elopement unplanned, they'd relied on their photographer to decide on the location for their ceremony. "I was so overcome with emotion when our photographer led us there, because he didn't even know," she says, referring to her fondness for the gardens.

"Florence has so much history for us, and in our very biased opinion, is one of the most magical places on earth—in part because of its beauty and history, but mostly because it's where we found each other. There wasn't another place our wedding could've been that made sense for us."

Katelyn & Carlos's Fine Print

LIVE: Glendale, California

WORK: Katelyn is a marketing and business development manager, and Carlos is a film and television producer.

AGES WHEN THEY ELOPED: She was twenty-nine, and he was twenty-seven.

KATELYN'S FIRST IMPRESSION: "Honestly, I was kind of concerned for Carlos when we met at the airport! He looked a little glossed over and was super stoic in a terminal full of people literally running on adrenaline. . . . But there was also a part of me—a really large part of me—that was really into that mysterious, handsome man-vibe he had going on."

CARLOS'S FIRST IMPRESSION: "A woman on a mission. Although to be fair, everyone seems like that to me when I'm traveling, especially in an airport."

RELATIONSHIP TIME LINE: Dated for eight years → Engaged for a little more than eighteen months → Eloped August 2018 → Honeymooned September 2018

WEDDING VENUE: The Boboli Gardens

DISTANCE FROM HOME TO VENUE: 6,183 miles / 9,951 km

NUMBER OF GUESTS: 0

SHE WORE: A circa-2014 Sarah Seven dress from Still White (an online pre-owned wedding dress store) and metallic braided sandals

HE WORE: A midnight-blue tuxedo from Friar Tux, a custom shirt from Proper Cloth, shoes from Vintage Foundry Co., and Brooks Brothers Dalmatian Cuff Links, which look like their Australian shepherd—their way of including her

SOMETHING BORROWED AND BLUE: Katelyn's mother lent Katelyn her wedding garter, which was white lace with a blue ribbon running through it.

VOWS: The day before their ceremony, Katelyn and Carlos stopped at Giulio Giannini e Figlio, a historic papermaker near Pitti Palace on the south side of the Arno River, and purchased hand-marbled cards for their vows. They wrote them the day of their ceremony, apart from each other, "and somehow both ended up writing some of the same things, verbatim," says Katelyn.

SPENT: $13,883 for the wedding and honeymoon

BIGGEST SPLURGE: They spent almost half of their budget on their photographer. "It was important to us that if we were going to have only one record of our day that had to serve as the eyes for all of our family, that record would be beautiful and comprehensive, and the photographer a good fit to our personalities and aesthetics," says Katelyn. "We now have this gorgeous, incredibly detailed record of our wedding, and the amazing thing is, we were able to be so in the moment that we don't remember taking most of the photos. Even our families felt like they were there."

WHAT THEY DID WITH THE MONEY THEY SAVED: Put it toward a trip to Oahu to celebrate their first anniversary

How to Pull Off a Destination Elopement Abroad

To those who feel that it's not a true elopement until the seatbelt sign dings off and you're left with a slight twinge of anxiety that the coffeepot's still on, here's what to know as you head for a textbook elopement abroad (and please, *relax*).

Get Legally Married at Home First

Straight up, it is tedious, compli-cated, and expensive to get legally married overseas. For instance, France requires proof of residency by one partner for forty days in the city where you want the legal ceremony to take place. You need a significant number of legal docu-ments and many need to be trans-lated into French. And since France is a secular country, you must have a civil ceremony performed by a French authority prior to a religious ceremony (if that's your wish).

Ready to move on? Good.

> If you do decide to brave a civil ceremony overseas, it's in your best interest to hire a wedding planner who lives in your destination to guide you through the process, translate the paperwork, and ensure your union is legal in that country.

To keep things simple, low stress, and inexpensive, just hold a civil ceremony at the courthouse before your overseas elopement. Once at your destination, hold a sym-bolic ceremony, where you can exchange wedding rings and say your vows (which feels far more romantic when there's no paperwork to stress about). And you can have whomever you want perform the ceremony. Or no one at all. (Whether you keep any of this a secret is up to you.)

THE RULES OF PACKING

1. *Do not* pack your dress or suit in your checked luggage. Check with your airline to see whether they allow wedding attire in the flight attendant's coat closet on the plane. If not, or if there's no room, politely ask those around you if you can lay your garment bag on top of their luggage in the overhead compartment.

2. For the wedding bands, you might think it's responsible of you to put them in your carry-on. It's not checked luggage, right? Wrong. If you put your carry-on in the overhead compartment, it could get stolen. If it's beneath your seat, it could slide away. These are extreme scenarios, yes, but not entirely unfathomable. When traveling with rings, most jewelers recommend keeping them on you. Pin them inside your pocket and give security a heads-up. This is not a novel situation for them.

If you're planning to propose on your trip, pin the engagement ring in your pocket. Follow your partner through security. When you step into the full-body scanner, mouth to the security office that there's an engagement ring in your pocket and point to it. They'll discreetly pat you down and send you through with a knowing nod.

Destination Elopement Checklist

- Check to see whether your passport is expired, and take into consideration that there should be at least three to six months before it expires to be safe.

- Make photocopies of passports, driver's licenses, and credit cards. (When you reach your destination, lock your passports in the room's safe and carry copies on you when you're out touristing. The copies are crucial should your passports or other cards get stolen.)

- Exchange money for the local currency at your bank ahead of time—going through your bank means you avoid fees from airport kiosks or foreign ATMs.

- Give your credit card companies a heads-up that you're heading to a foreign country, and look into which ones charge foreign transaction fees. Don't use those.

- Research the electrical outlet type that's standard where you're headed, and buy the necessary adaptors (one for each of you).

- Download a good language app, one that at least teaches you how to say common phrases.

As discussed in the previous chapter, find and hire your vendors well in advance. Either take vendors with you to your destination or hire them locally. Whichever you choose, make sure they have extensive experience working in your destination.

Top 5 Elopement Destinations for Getting Your Passport Stamped

Classic European

Paris with an Intimate Twist

Oh, Paris, you magical city. There's a lot to love about the French capital—endless sidewalk cafés, picnics with baguettes and wine on the Eiffel Tower lawn, strolls on cobblestone streets while admiring all the pretty painted doors in Le Marais (hand-in-hand, of course)—and we refuse to apologize for embracing every Parisian cliché. That's all part of the fun.

Paris is rife with romantic photo ops, but to avoid the crowds at your actual ceremony, why not say your vows in one of Paris's many intimate gardens nestled throughout the city's twenty arrondissements, and save the Eiffel Tower for portrait shots instead? Here are a few of our favorites.

PARC MONCEAU

Located in Paris's chic 8th arrondissement, Parc Monceau is best known (and beloved) for its charming, photogenic bridge, which is modeled after the Rialto Bridge in Venice and is an obvious choice for where to say your vows. Although the bridge is accessible all year-round, plan an autumn elopement to capture vibrant foliage in your photos.

SQUARE DU VERT-GALANT

Despite sitting right in the middle of Paris on the River Seine, Square du Vert-Galant remains relatively isolated, an ideal spot for a quiet

POSITANO: THE DARLING OF THE AMALFI COAST

Beneath those stacked, blush-colored houses that cling to the cliffs of the Amalfi Coast lies the village of Positano. While small, it offers a variety of spots for elopements, none more romantic than centuries-old hotels with private, candlelit courtyards. Spiaggia Grande (the main beach) is just a five-minute walk away from most hotels, where you can also say your vows as the Mediterranean stretches out before you.

Getting there: Book a private car service at Naples International Airport. The Amalfi Coast is known for many things, but easy driving is not one of them thanks to its steep and twisting cobblestone roads. A car service will get you there cheaper than a cab would.

If you have time before your ceremony, take the hour-long bus ride to the actual town of Amalfi, which is best known for producing handmade paper following ancient Italian tradition. Visit the Amatruda paper mill, the only mill still operating in Amalfi, to pick up the thick, soft paper called bambagina, which you can use to write your vows on.

Don't miss: It's touristy, yes, but don't skip a boat ride; this is how you'll get the money shot of those pretty houses on the cliffs. If your skill set includes driving boats, rent a Zodiac, a small but zippy rubber motorboat, and ride up the coast to the town of Furore, located in the Campania region of Italy, where an enormous fjord opens up to a dreamy hidden beach that's perfect for a picnic lunch.

Or hop the ferry to the nearby Isle of Capri and take the chairlift to Monte Solaro for sweeping views of the Mediterranean, then head back down to Piazza Umberto, the glamorous pulse of the island. Though small, the outdoor square is the place to see and be seen on the island (and drink an Aperol Spritz worth a small fortune).

When to go: Aim to visit in the spring or fall (May and September are ideal) to avoid the summer onslaught of tourists that cram the beaches.

Addio!

---

elopement. You'll be surrounded by weeping willows and Bohemian olive trees, with the Louvre peeking through in the background.

PARC DE BAGATELLE

For a truly hidden gem, seek out Parc de Bagatelle in the Bois de Boulogne. Not only is its gazebo overlooking a rose garden the perfect intimate venue, but it's also one of Paris's four botanical gardens, home to tiny bridges, caves(!), and a nineteenth-century Chinese pagoda.

WHEN TO GO:

March to May and September to October. High season hits in June and July, when throngs of tourists descend on the City of Lights, meaning high rates and crowded parks. Instead, head to Paris during its "shoulder seasons," which refer to the spring or fall months when you'll find cheaper rates, pleasant temps, and fewer lines at the top tourist spots.

5 MORE CLASSIC EUROPEAN CITIES TO ELOPE TO:

- Barcelona, Spain
- Lisbon, Portugal
- London, England
- Rome, Italy
- Vienna, Austria

WHERE EUROPEANS ELOPE IN EUROPE

If you're seeking something a little more under-the-radar (translation: more affordable and less touristy), here's where in-the-know Europeans go to elope.

- Algarve, Portugal
- Valletta, Malta
- Monte Carlo, Monaco
- Rhodes, Greece
- Dubrovnik, Croatia

Iconic Cities Around the Globe

Sydney

Considered not only one of the most iconic cities in the world, but one of the most livable too, Sydney has a reputation as a top destination stemming from its golden beaches, vibrant urban scene, and chill locals with a welcoming vibe. (It's not unusual for visitors to strongly consider moving there.) The coastal city's crown jewels are inarguably the Sydney Harbour Bridge and the Sydney Opera House, both of which grace Sydney Harbour, itself a glistening attraction for tourists and locals alike. The harbor is edged with fine dining and casual restaurants, boutique hotels, the Taronga Zoo (which is open 365 days a year), and ample public spaces for elopements—you'll find an abundance of waterfront piers, landings, and parks, and many are free to use (but be sure to check with the local council on permit requirements and bookings). For the least amount of unwanted passersby, aim for a weekday elopement at sunrise or sunset.

If a low-stress waterfront elopement only steps from the bustle of the city sounds ideal, here are some top spots to choose from.

CAPTAIN HENRY WATERHOUSE RESERVE

Located near the base of the Sydney Harbour Bridge, with spectacular views of the Opera House across the harbor, Captain Henry Waterhouse Reserve is a beautiful park and an optimal location for a waterfront elopement ceremony. Its flat expanse allows for easy seating (should you have guests) and decorative touches, such as arches and aisle runners, which many local elopement companies provide. The reserve also offers the unique opportunity for arrival and departure by boat or water taxi.

ON A BOAT

For those seeking truly panoramic views, the best way to take in the city is by boat, and it cannot be overstated how major the boat scene is in Sydney, thanks to the harbor's beckoning waters. The absolute plethora of boating options for elopements includes yachts, cruise boats, pontoon boats, and sailboats. Most are priced by the hour, and some allow for overnight stays.

THE ROYAL BOTANIC GARDEN SYDNEY

The Royal Botanic Garden is an oasis wrapping more than 74 acres around Sydney Harbour. Established in 1816, it's the oldest scientific institution in the country, home to rare plants, elegant pavilions, and a rose garden that blooms from September to May, as well as a dozen unique spots for tying the knot, many of which sit right on the water. The primo spot is Bennelong Lawn, which neighbors the Sydney Opera House and provides stunning bridge views. Sitting a bit more inland, the garden's Palm House & Lawn is home to the oldest glasshouse in New South Wales. For more privacy in the outdoors, Tarpeian Lawn is favored for its peacefulness and, though shaded by fig trees, still offers picturesque views.

SAWMILLERS RESERVE

If you're looking for something more secluded, Sawmillers Reserve is a hidden waterfront gem. The site of a centuries-old timber yard, the land was developed in the 1980s into a reserve by modernist landscape architect Harry Howard. Follow the winding steps down to the water's edge for the best shots, where you'll also find the remains of a shipwreck.

5 MORE ICONIC CITIES TO ELOPE TO

- Bangkok, Thailand
- Cape Town, South Africa
- Rio de Janeiro, Brazil
- Mexico City, Mexico
- Tokyo, Japan

Outdoor Adventure

Iceland: The Land of Fire, Ice, and Lebowski

If your hopes and dreams include eloping on an island of active volcanoes in below-freezing temps, pack your headlamp and head to Iceland. This North Atlantic island hasn't just quietly emerged as one of the most popular elopement spots in the world—it has straight-up eclipsed them. In 2019, the only European elopement destination more popular was Paris.

Why? For one, its diverse array of geography—waterfalls, black sand beaches strewn with diamond-like chunks of ice, electric blue lagoons—makes for breathtaking elopements. Plus, Iceland's compact size (it could fit neatly inside the state of Colorado) makes exploring it achievable with a rental car in just a few days.

Beyond its natural wonders are obscurities too. On the south coast of the Snæfellsnes Peninsula you'll find a tiny, one-room black church named Búðakirkja, which sits atop a lava field. It is—you guessed it—quite popular for elopements.

Not to be outdone by Mother Nature, Iceland's capital, Reykjavik, offers its own gift: the Lebowski Bar. The bar's interior is divided into four separate themes—a bowling alley, a Southern-style porch, a 1950s diner, and a 1960s playboy lounge—all of which can be rented out for your elopement. We'll raise a White Russian to *that*.

WHEN TO GO:

September to December. The fall is off-season in Iceland, meaning thinner crowds and roadways. Yes, you'll be facing 30°F [-1°C] temps, but this is *the* best time of year to see the northern lights, which are most commonly spotted between 9:30 p.m. and 1 a.m. thanks to a mere six hours of daylight. If you're thinking of going in December, aim for early in the month, before holiday festivities draw in tourists.

5 MORE ADVENTUROUS PLACES TO ELOPE TO

- Banff, Alberta, Canada
- Nosara, Costa Rica
- Dolomite Mountains, Italy
- Patagonia, Argentina
- Queenstown, New Zealand

Tropical Getaway

Bali: An Island of Options

One of the roughly seventeen thousand islands in the Indonesian archipelago, Bali offers more than just white (and black) sand beaches. Known as the "Island of the Gods," Bali has become a top destination for tropical island elopements. Beyond its more than forty beaches,

Bali offers a cornucopia of spots to say "I do": towering waterfalls, lush jungles, dramatic cliffs, and active volcanoes. There's plenty to explore, from its ancient temples and palaces to the Coral Triangle, situated on the northeastern edge of the peninsula, which has the highest diversity of marine species on earth. Build in a day of snorkeling to take in the spectacular subterranean sights.

BEACHES

First off, if you're heading to Bali to get married with the surf at your feet, know that most of its beaches are public, and *not* owned by the five-star oceanfront hotels that hulk beyond the sand. You'll find more privacy (and less photobombing) at Sanur Beach, Crystal Bay, and Jimbaran Beach on the island's southern peninsula. Looking for black sand beaches? Head to Keramas Beach on the east coast, where volcanic eruptions have created onyx sand that shimmers with mica. The beach is largely untouched by tourists, who flock to the west coast for surfing and sunsets, but you'll need to hire a driver to get there, as it's not accessible by public transportation.

WATERFALLS

To the north of Ubud you'll find Nungnung Waterfall, which has the highest altitude of any of the falls on the island and is located in Petang Village. To get to the waterfall, you'll descend 509 steps, which takes around twenty minutes (going back up takes thirty to forty-five). When you arrive, you'll see a huge fall with water plunging 165 feet [50 m] to a pool below. Know that the sound of water crashing at this volume is described as "thunderous," so it might be a bit harder to hear one another as you say your vows. Wear clothes that dry quickly, as you're likely to get misted.

If you'd like a toes-in-the-shallow-pool kind of ceremony, head to Tibumana Waterfall, located in Bangli Village. It's more secluded than Nungnung and will have far fewer tourists. It's accessible from a parking lot via bamboo bridges.

If ever a waterfall could be called a "hidden gem," it'd be the Tukad Cepung Waterfall. Located inside a cove, it's more difficult to access than the others, and can only be reached by squeezing through narrow passageways between rocks. The effort is worth it to see water cascading into the cove from a green forest canopy above, along with streams of sunlight that create a photographer's dream outdoor studio.

If you're going the waterfall route, plan to wear sandals with decent grip and your bathing suit under your attire (or just your suit) for a celebratory, post-ceremony dip.

CLIFFS

A top spot for nuptials, Balangan Cliff rises six stories high over the Indian Ocean on the western edge of Bali's Bukit Peninsula. It's accessible by car (there's parking nearby), and is a super popular place for elopements, both in spite of and because of its hidden location. Due to this demand, many local wedding and elopement companies offer packages, nearly all of which provide the hallmark of a Balangan Cliff ceremony: a floral arch that perfectly frames the sunset.

Many other Bali cliff tops have been taken over by villas, which you have to work with to gain access. It'll cost you, but you're guaranteed an intimate, private experience.

A NOTE ON (ACTIVE) VOLCANOES

If volcanoes aren't your thing, know that Bali sits on the Pacific Ocean's "Ring of Fire," where tectonic plates often shift; when they collide, they cause volcanic activity. Mount Agung, Bali's highest point at 9,444 feet [2,879 m], last erupted in 2019, which closed the airport and wreaked havoc on all aspects of travel—including those coming into the country to elope.

However, if you do fancy the idea of getting married standing atop churning lava, Mount Batur, located northwest of Mount Agung, has become a popular destination for elopements; at 5,633 feet [1,717 m], it's more hike-friendly. Many guides suggest doing a sunrise trek to the top, where you're rewarded with some of the island's most jaw-dropping views of sunrise. (Just know that it's also an active volcano.)

WHEN TO GO:

April and September. The busiest season is the dry season, June to August, so to avoid crowded beaches and heavy traffic, the early spring and fall bring warm temps with less humidity and fewer tourists. Hate monsoons? Avoid visiting between October and March, when Bali is drenched in wind-fueled downpours.

- Puerto Vallarta, Mexico
- Seychelle Islands, East Africa
- St. Lucia, Caribbean
- Tahiti, French Polynesia
- Airlie Beach, Australia

In December 1981, Barbara and Leonard Barnes became the first couple to get married at Sandals Montego Bay, Jamaica, with staff members standing in as maid of honor and best man. Sandals and its ten thousand weddings per year have obviously stood the test of time—as has Barbara and Leonard's marriage. In the summer of 2019, Leonard saved Barbara's life by giving her one of his kidneys. To celebrate their lasting love, Sandals hosted a vow renewal ceremony and reception for the couple at its revamped Montego Bay location later that fall.

Snowy Wonderland

Quebec City, Quebec

The capital city of Quebec is at its most enchanting in the winter. Old Quebec, the historic and cultural heart of Quebec City, turns into a real-life holiday card displaying delicate snowfall, wintry strolls on cobblestone roads, twinkling lights, and plenty of hot cocoa. Old Quebec was settled by the French more than four hundred years ago (called "New France" at the time) and today offers European charm without the transatlantic flight.

Visit in February for the Winter Carnival, held to warm everyone's hearts during the long cold months, figuratively and literally. There's a slew of outdoor activities, including a night parade, ice canoe races, and ice sculpting. Revelers imbibe copious amounts of the official party drink, Caribou, a deep red punch that clocks in at 22.9 percent alcohol, its recipe a trade secret.

CHÂTEAU FRONTENAC HOTEL

Said to be the most photographed hotel in the world, Château Frontenac Hotel rests high on a bluff overlooking the St. Lawrence River. It is a grand display of opulent Victorian architecture, holding

610 rooms. The historic hotel was finished in 1893 and has been visited by royals including Princess Grace of Monaco and Queen Elizabeth II. Today, the luxury estate offers intimate ceremony and elopement packages with varying tiers of options for accommodations, portrait sessions, and even live music from a professional violinist.

DUFFERIN TERRACE

This long, wooden boardwalk below Château Frontenac Hotel and above the St. Lawrence River turns into a splendid white canvas in the winter. Don a faux fur muff and cape and get married inside one of the terrace's five elegant gazebos, then head for an experience not to be missed: a toboggan slide that shoots you down the hillside and offers sweeping views of the city. At the bottom, grab some beavertails—flat pieces of sweetened fried dough—from a kiosk, or sample maple syrup snacks from a sugar shack.

MONTGOMERY FALLS

Just a twenty-minute drive from Quebec City, Montgomery Falls is a towering spectacle of nature that becomes even more ethereal in the winter, when the falls turn to ice and the pool of water below becomes a quiet tundra. Montgomery Falls is one of the tallest in Canada, besting Niagara Falls by 99 feet [30 m] to reach a height of 272 feet [83 m]. Say your vows on the suspension bridge that stretches across the entire width of the falls at the crest, or, if you're feeling adventurous, snowshoe to the foot of the falls, where your only company is likely to be the ice climbers above.

WHEN TO GO:

December to February. It will be brisk—Quebec City is one of the coldest places in North America. December is surprisingly not too crowded and holds all the holiday cheer you could ever want. If you're on a budget, plan to go after the New Year, when hotel prices drop significantly. And, if you don't mind swarms of people, time it for the Winter Carnival.

5 MORE SNOWY WONDERLAND PLACES TO ELOPE TO

- Bavarian Alps, Germany
- Bergen, Norway
- Gstaad, Switzerland
- Prague, Czech Republic
- Sapporo, Japan

De

stination
USA

RaeAnn & Nick

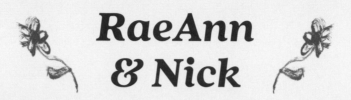

For RaeAnn, the decision to choose a hiking elopement came easy. She had seen photos of them floating around on Instagram, and since she and Nick had been talking about getting married pretty frequently, she mentioned it to him. He liked the idea, so they ran with it.

Both RaeAnn and Nick are in the Army and had to squeeze in their elopement before he shipped out for basic training. Since he was stationed in Arlington, Virginia, at the time, they secured a local photographer who helped steer them toward choosing Cole Mountain for their elopement, just a few hours south.

While RaeAnn's family was supportive of their elopement plans from the get-go, Nick's parents were not. "It was really hard for me," RaeAnn says. "I'd never had someone's parents not like me. I felt awful that my fiancé's parents seemed to disapprove of us."

But, she says, they both knew what they wanted—a low-cost, no-frills, intimate wedding, "something that celebrated what it was really about in a way that was very 'us.'"

The day of their hike, they drove to the trailhead, changed into wedding attire in the dirt parking lot, and headed up the mountain with their photographer in tow. In lieu of an officiant, they played a sermon they'd had their Bible study leader record on Nick's phone.

Then, they read their vows from little booklets they gave each other. "Our vows that we each wrote were for each other," says RaeAnn. "To me, expression of that love and the promises I would make were for Nick alone. I didn't want to feel uncomfortable or limited in what to say."

After the hike, they headed to a nearby rental house that "we may or may not have chosen because it had the channel we needed to watch the Packers-Bears game," she says (they're die-hard Packers fans). They celebrated with one of their favorite things to eat, a charcuterie board, which they'd prepped the night before with meats and cheeses from Whole Foods. They toasted with their favorite beer, Apricot Blonde from Dry Rock Brewing Co., "and had the best, stress-free evening," says RaeAnn. "It was very casual, but again, perfect for us." To top off the day, the Packers won, 24–23.

Together they decided to put their elopement on social media before it was RaeAnn's turn to leave for basic training. Then, that Christmas, they sent out "Merry Christmas from the Fahnrichs!" cards featuring some of their wedding photos. For their parents, they took advantage of a Shutterfly discount and made photobooks that included details about their day. Says RaeAnn, "It felt like a good way to let them see our day, and more special than just sharing digital photos."

She eventually came to peace with how Nick's parents felt. "I know that his family is very traditional, and that they would have preferred for us to have a traditional wedding, but I stand by our decision to make our wedding ours and to commit ourselves to each other in the way that we did. It was intimate and beautiful, and it was just so perfect for us. I was sad about the lack of support, but I would do it again because it was the perfect choice for us.

"And his family came around about a month later, so if anyone else experiences that, just wait it out and stick to making your 'I do' your dream 'I do'—I would have regretted it any other way!"

RaeAnn & Nick's Fine Print

LIVE: Arlington, Virginia

WORK: RaeAnn is an officer in the US Army and Nick is an infantryman in the Army.

AGES WHEN THEY ELOPED: She was twenty-four, and he was twenty-two.

RAEANN'S FIRST IMPRESSION: "When I first saw Nick I remember thinking that he was attractive. I remember that he had a big laugh (he still does) and a distinct walk, more of a strut to be honest, but he'll deny that he walks abnormally. He was funny and seemed silly but was still able to carry a meaningful political conversation. One minute we were talking about the pros and cons of presidential candidates and their economic policies and the next we were laughing so hard I could barely breathe. Talking to him was easy, and he made me feel happy and calm."

NICK'S FIRST IMPRESSION: "I remember that [RaeAnn] gave a speech in her red dress with her hair up, and she was really pretty."

RELATIONSHIP TIME LINE: Dated for two years → Engaged for one month → Courthouse elopement August 2018 → Hiking elopement September 2018

PROPOSAL: Says RaeAnn: "We talked about getting married for a while before we actually got engaged. We both knew that it was what we wanted. At Nick's 'family weekend' for basic training [in Georgia], he told me that he intended to get me a ring the next day. Even though I knew it was coming, Nick still took me to the River Walk in Columbus, Georgia, and we found a secluded gazebo where he proposed on July 29, 2018."

WEDDING VENUE: Cole Mountain, Virginia

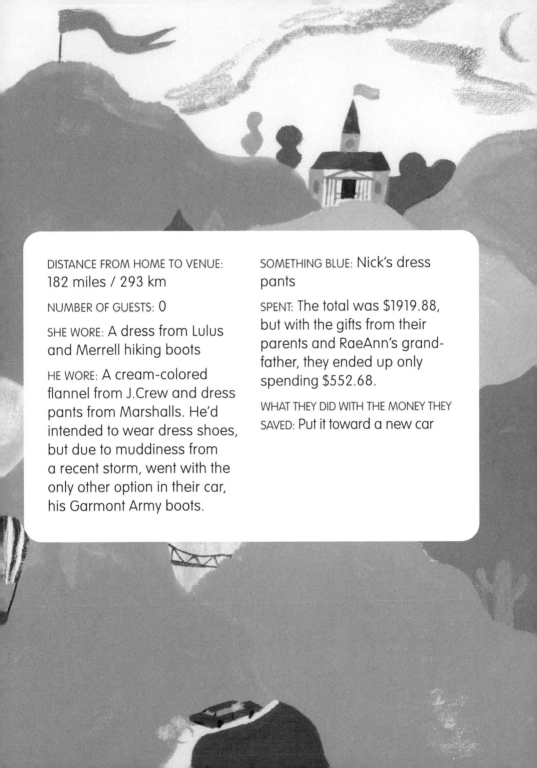

DISTANCE FROM HOME TO VENUE:
182 miles / 293 km

NUMBER OF GUESTS: 0

SHE WORE: A dress from Lulus and Merrell hiking boots

HE WORE: A cream-colored flannel from J.Crew and dress pants from Marshalls. He'd intended to wear dress shoes, but due to muddiness from a recent storm, went with the only other option in their car, his Garmont Army boots.

SOMETHING BLUE: Nick's dress pants

SPENT: The total was $1919.88, but with the gifts from their parents and RaeAnn's grand-father, they ended up only spending $552.68.

WHAT THEY DID WITH THE MONEY THEY SAVED: Put it toward a new car

Keep It Continental

A destination elopement doesn't have to involve jet lag or early check-in. If your idea of eloping involves a good, windows-down road trip or a layover-free flight, read on for some of the best destinations the United States has to offer (and no, we didn't forget about Las Vegas—in fact, we're giving it the full treatment in chapter 5).

Destination USA: Best-of Edition

Urban: Chicago

As the third largest city in America, it should come as no surprise that Chicago has countless features that make it great for eloping. Each of the city's many urban neighborhoods provides a totally unique experience—from the nightlife in Boystown, to the vintage shops and coffeehouses in Wicker Park, to the excellent dining in Little Italy. Architecturally, the city is gorgeous, filled with Art Deco skyscrapers and brownstone row houses that'll make excellent backdrops to your portraits, plus plenty of refurbished industrial spots and spectacular boutique hotels. As for entertainment, in addition to dining at Chicago's many Michelin-starred restaurants, the city is home to a world-class orchestra, opera, and museums (the Art Institute and the Field Museum are must-sees), excellent shopping along the Magnificent Mile, plus a calendar chock-full of street festivals during the warmer months.

BEST TIME TO VISIT:

June through October. While in most of the United States spring starts in late March, Chicago winters stretch far later into the year. (It's not all that uncommon for snow to fall in May. Yes, May.) Stick to June through October, when the bright summer sun warms the city, only to be cooled down by the pleasant lakefront breezes.

PRO TIP:

In late September, thousands of runners will take over Lake Shore Drive for the Chicago Half

Marathon, and in mid-October, be prepared for lots of street closures to accommodate the Chicago Marathon. Should you brave it out to visit in March, keep in mind that Chicago goes big for St. Paddy's Day, with a huge parade and a green-dyed Chicago River. And in early August, the massive annual music festival Lollapalooza takes over Grant Park, hosting around 400,000 attendees annually, so be prepared for the crowds (and high demand on hotel rooms).

TOP ELOPEMENT SPOT:

McCormick Bridgehouse & Chicago River Museum. For a downtown elopement that's right in the thick of the action, head to McCormick Bridgehouse, a five-story mini-tower located right on the end of one of Chicago's famous moving bridges. From inside the museum, you'll get 360-degree views of the Chicago River and surrounding city. Their (very reasonable) by-the-hour rental fees allow you to book the 1,200-square-foot [111 square-metre] industrial space inside the museum (think: lots of exposed bricks and steel beams), which also comes with access to the museum's private Riverwalk plaza. If the weather is playing nice, you can say your vows on the plaza in the open air.

5 MORE URBAN DESTINATIONS TO ELOPE TO

- Denver, Colorado
- Miami, Florida
- Nashville, Tennessee
- New York, New York
- Portland, Oregon

5 BEST SMALL CITIES TO ELOPE TO

- Carmel, California
- New Hope, Pennsylvania
- Old Town Alexandria, Virginia
- Savannah, Georgia
- St. Augustine, Florida

5 UNDERRATED CITIES TO ELOPE TO

- Madison, Wisconsin
- Pittsburgh, Pennsylvania
- Portland, Maine
- Richmond, Virginia
- St. Louis, Missouri

Coastal: Key West

Thanks to it being the southern-most city in the contiguous United States, Key West is practically a stone's throw from the Caribbean and the laid-back, tropical vibes that accompany it. There's a party every night in the island city, so kick off your elopement festivities by joining the regular crew of revelers in Old Town's Mallory Square come sunset. Then, hit famous Duval Street, which stretches from the Gulf of Mexico to the Atlantic Ocean and is infamous for its more than three dozen bars (and bar crawl). At the bottom of the island, you'll find the iconic sign marking mile 0, the very beginning of US 1—and perhaps the very beginning of a brand-new chapter in love.

BEST TIME TO VISIT:

March through May. This springtime window is sandwiched nicely between Key West's high season for tourists and hurricane season. During winter months, an onslaught of regular snowbirds and first-time visitors seeking the heat will crowd beaches and hotels, kicking up the price tag. Throughout the summer and into fall, there's always the risk of a tropical storm or hurricane (technically, that season runs from June to November). Stick to spring.

PRO TIP:

If an extravagant costume party is the wild, energetic backdrop you envision for your elopement, consider a visit during Key West's Fantasy Fest. But otherwise, steer clear of October. For ten days stretching over the two weekends before Halloween, the city throws more than sixty parties, masked marches, and street fairs, culminating in a massive parade. And make no mistake: It's far from tame. Public nudity, X-rated costumes, and appearances by adult-film stars are the norm. If that's your vibe, it might be just the thing to spice up your big day—but if not, consider yourself warned.

TOP ELOPEMENT SPOT:

Fort Zachary Taylor Historic State Park. Part Civil War fort, part striking beach, and part wildlife reserve, Fort Zachary Taylor Historic State Park comprises a 54-acre National Historic Landmark at the tip of Key West, where the Atlantic Ocean and the Gulf of Mexico meet. It's a stunning option for a toes-in-the-sand ceremony— hit the east side for sunrise and the west for sunset—and in between, devote at least an afternoon to exploring the rest of its wonders. The island's flora and fauna are at

their peak in the park: Trek along one of two nature trails in the area to discover native wildflowers and the area's best bird-watching, or take in the underwater ecosystem while snorkeling among a rainbow of coral.

5 MORE COASTAL DESTINATIONS TO ELOPE TO

- Big Sur, California
- Cannon Beach, Oregon
- Kauai, Hawaii
- Newport, Rhode Island
- Outer Banks, North Carolina

Lake: Lake Tahoe

The allure of Lake Tahoe stems from its sparkling waters and mountainous backdrops, but it's the lake's location that makes it a top draw for elopers. It shares a border with two states—Nevada to the east and California to the west—but the real divide is between North Lake (Tahoe City to Incline Village) and South Lake (Emerald Bay to Zephyr Cove). The former, mostly in California and more of a locals' hideaway, will deliver a serene, nature-filled elopement. Stargaze, kayak, or snowshoe the days away, then hit one of the area's two ale trails, the North Lake Tahoe Ale Trail or the South Lake Tahoe Beer Trail, before retreating to a private lodge. Cross the lake by boat shuttle (or circle around it by car), and the scene shifts: The south shore is mostly in Nevada and feels more like if a ski-resort town had a baby with Vegas—nightlife galore (casinos! bars! clubs!).

BEST TIME TO VISIT:

May to June and September to November. While Tahoe averages three hundred days of sunshine, the slim shoulder season between late spring and early summer is prime time for good weather. Snow lingers through March, and late-season squalls are common in April, but when May rolls around, temps rise to comfortable 60s and 70s [16°C–26°C], and precipitation drops off. By June, most days are gorgeous, and warm-weather activities are in full swing—hiking, kayaking, paddleboarding, lying on the beach.

As summer progresses, though, crowds fill hotels, and prices and traffic soar before dropping off come September, when the lake also warms to comfortable temps for a dip. Summer crowds thin out, making the early fall months ideal for an elopement at one of the popular viewpoints.

For winter lovers, Lake Tahoe is magical come November (hence Tahoe's fifteen beloved ski resorts). Blanketing the area's forests and mountains, the heavy snowfall turns the already beautiful setting into a scene plucked from a snow globe—just make sure you have a vehicle with four-wheel drive and snow tires for navigating the area.

PRO TIP:

The period between Christmas and New Year's will be one of the most expensive weeks to visit Tahoe, as it corresponds with time off from work and school and hits during peak powder season for skiers and snowboarders. If you're set on a winter elopement, aim for a few weeks before the holidays, or in January—when the north shore's ski resorts offer specials for newbies—to secure the best rates.

TOP ELOPEMENT SPOT:

Logan Shoals Vista Point. Sunset seekers, take note: The eastern shore's Logan Shoals Vista Point beautifully frames the setting sun behind the lake and the mountains to the west. Host an early-evening ceremony at the rocky outcropping or the paved resting area with stone benches, then head north on the footpath to shoot portraits atop granite boulders before twilight. What's more, these vantage points are easily accessible with a short walk from a free parking lot off Highway 50, just north of Cave Rock. Because the land falls under the jurisdiction of the US Forest Service, however, you'll be required to use one of the wedding-service providers that holds a Special Use Permit.

5 MORE LAKE DESTINATIONS TO ELOPE TO

- Finger Lakes, New York
- Flathead Lake, Montana
- Lake Nockamixon, Pennsylvania
- Portage Lake, Alaska
- Ross Lake, Washington

Mountain/Forest: National Parks

Elopements in US national parks have surged in popularity over the last decade, so much so that it's not uncommon to come across elegantly dressed couples waiting in line for *the* shot. If your adventurous spirit is set on marrying in a national park, here's what to know as you plan.

- Visit the National Park Service website for the specific park you're planning to elope to and fill out an application for a Special Use Permit. These permits can range from $50 to $200.

- Research the locations within the park where wedding ceremonies and wedding photography are permitted depending on your guest count—most national parks offer a wider variety of locations for small parties.

- Check whether your photographer already has the proper permit to shoot there (if applicable—some parks only require a photography permit if the photos will be used commercially). If not, it's good form to cover the cost of the photography permit.

- Read up on the rules—you are on government property, after all.

- Know the vehicle limit for your location and carpool when possible.

- Do not disturb the natural ecology of the area: Only use flowers that are native to the environment or are hardy and will not drop seeds; don't throw birdseed or release butterflies; and stay on the trail.

- Bring your permit with you the day of your ceremony. Be prepared to also pay admissions or parking fees—another reason carpooling is a good idea if you're bringing guests.

- If you pop Champagne to get *the* shot (you know which one), go find that cork!

PRO TIP:

Some parks have seen such high volumes of weddings that popular spots have become destroyed. Please, *please* respect Mother Nature, and do not venture off the trail for the sake of an epic shot. Consider donating to the National Park Service to show your gratitude for being able to use the land for your personal use.

THE 10 MOST POPULAR NATIONAL PARKS FOR ELOPEMENTS

1. Yosemite National Park, California

2. Joshua Tree National Park, California

3. Rocky Mountain National Park, Colorado

4. Zion National Park, Utah

5. Glacier National Park, Montana

6. Grand Teton National Park, Wyoming

7. Grand Canyon National Park, Arizona

8. Mount Rainier National Park, Washington

9. Olympic National Park, Washington

10. Shenandoah National Park, Virginia

Things to Bring on a Hiking Elopement

- Hiking boots
- Change of clothes
- Extra hoodie or sweater
- Rain jacket
- Snacks/water/bubbly/beer (don't forget a bottle opener or corkscrew and cups, plates, napkins, etc.)
- A blanket for the above picnic you'll be having
- Headlamp or flashlight
- Paper map of the park (in case you lose cell service)
- Waterproof matches or a lighter, just in case

5 GREAT MOUNTAIN AND FOREST DESTINATIONS THAT AREN'T NATIONAL PARKS

- Asheville, North Carolina
- Burlington, Vermont
- Ouray, Colorado
- Promise Ridge, Pennsylvania
- Savage River State Forest, Maryland

Desert: Palm Springs, California

Nestled beneath Southern California's San Jacinto Mountains, Palm Springs is a mecca for eloping couples from all over the world. Besides the fact that it sees three hundred fifty days of sunshine each year, it's also brimming with diverse excursions that go beyond the Sonoran Desert that it sits in. Take the Palm Springs Aerial Tram to hiking trails that lead to snow, find lush greenery alongside cacti in the highly photogenic Moorten Botanical Garden, or stay grounded and shop the rows of boutiques that sit on palm tree–lined streets. After a day in the sun, cool off at one of the area's fab hotel pools.

BEST TIME TO VISIT:

January through May. The year starts with temps in the 70s [20s Celsius] that climb to the mid-90s [30s] by May—then it's triple digits through September. Avoid November and December; while cooler, the city is incredibly busy with festivities.

PRO TIP:

One of the biggest music events of the year, the Coachella Valley Music and Arts Festival takes place every April at the Empire Polo Club in Indio, California, 30 miles [48 km] east of Palm Springs. On back-to-back, three-day weekends, thousands of fans from around the world descend on the area, clogging up highways for hundreds of miles and causing hotel rates to soar. Then, Stagecoach, a country music fest, piggybacks off Coachella for a third weekend of music and partying in the desert. This is either literal music to your elopement planning ears, or a month to be avoided at all costs.

TOP ELOPEMENT SPOT:

Palm Springs Visitors Center. OK, hear us out: The Palm Springs Visitors Center is not your standard run-of-the-mill pit stop—it's a striking display of modernist architecture characterized by its majestic, kite-shaped roof. Yes, when it opened in 1965 it was originally a gas station, but it was a *beautiful* one, because Swiss architect Albert Frey, who is regarded as a founding father of the city's "desert modernism" architectural style, designed it. In 2015, it was added to the National Register of Historic Places in recognition of its architectural significance. Today, It's your gateway to a desert elopement. It is located right off Highway 111 as you enter Palm Springs, and you can park your car at the center and use its bathrooms to ensure you're elopement-ready. Then, wander out into the open desert until you find a spot that makes your heart thump with "I dos."

5 MORE DESERT SPOTS TO ELOPE TO

- Apache Junction, Arizona
- Imperial Sand Dunes, California
- Marfa, Texas
- Moab, Utah
- Sonoran Desert, Arizona

THE VIRGIN ISLANDS, MILLENNIAL EDITION

If you swoon over sparkling turquoise water and your passport also happens to be expired, elope to St. Croix, which is part of the US Virgin Islands (hence no passport required). Skip the pricey beach elopement packages (that often come attached to pricey hotels) and head to Chenay Bay Beach for a more private ceremony. Say your vows next to the calmest, clearest waters on St. Croix, then head to Cruzan Rum Distillery to sample the sauce at the source. Stay at the bubblegum-pink Buccaneer Hotel, the oldest hotel on the island and home to Mermaid Beach, where you can relax on lounge chairs with more rum as the sunset melts into the horizon.

WHAT'S YOUR ELOPEMENT TYPE?

URBAN

Pros

Easy access to anything you may have forgotten in the hotel room (deodorant, cuff links, rings).

Ample photo ops—the grand staircase of the courthouse, a fountain in a park, murals, the skyline at sunset.

A wide range of dining options within walking (or Uber-ing) distance.

Heartwarming cheers from passersby.

Cons

Unwanted noise interrupting your vows—sirens, construction, squawking pigeons, heartwarming cheers from passersby.

Traffic or parking issues that can cause vendors, witnesses, or guests to run late.

More obstacles for photographers, which can lead to longer time spent taking photos (meaning goodbye to more of your money).

COASTAL

Pros

Your photos will be splendid. Go for both sunrise and sunset shots, and don't be afraid to get a little wet.

Book a rental house on the beach nearby for easy access to food, alcohol, outfit changes, a bathroom, and other accommodations.

Toes-in-the-sand ceremony.

Cons

There's a chance of inclement weather of the "natural disaster" variety.

If it's summer, expect sweat.

Sand. Everywhere.

Or mist. Everywhere.

LAKE

Pros

Lakeside elopements are great if you're having a few guests, as there's ample room to set out chairs, and the terrain is usually flat.

During the winter, you'll find reduced rates at many lakeside resorts, lodges, and rental homes.

Boating. Obviously.

Cons

Other people boating, Jet-Skiing, or audibly enjoying other nautical sports during your ceremony.

Mosquitoes, gnats, and horseflies all love lakes, so be OK with smelling faintly of bug spray all day.

Geese and ducks tend to congregate at lakes, so be on high alert for droppings (and expect honking).

MOUNTAINS/FOREST

Pros

True intimacy. Peace. Quiet.

Your photos will be insanely gorgeous thanks to endless photogenic backdrops courtesy of Mother Nature.

If hiking is involved, you'll get the satisfaction of having exercised on your wedding day.

Cons

If you go the white dress route, the hem will absolutely get dirty.

That whole lack of bathroom thing.

If your ceremony destination is strenuous to reach, plan on changing into your attire once you get there and touching up your hair and makeup too (meaning you'll have to carry everything with you).

DESERT

Pros

You're probably going to have the area all to yourselves.

The blank canvas that endless sand provides opens up opportunities to incorporate unique elements into your ceremony, such as a vintage rug.

Desert sunsets. That's all.

Cons

Let's start with the obvious: It's going to be very, very hot.

The nearest bathroom is likely to be . . . not close.

Walking on desert sand is difficult with shoes on. It's very hot without them.

CHAPTER 5:

Las Vegas

Lana & Ben

Six months after meeting her now-husband, Ben, at a speakeasy in Washington, DC, Lana took him with her on a business trip to Los Angeles. That led to a last-minute weekend trip to Las Vegas, which led to an elopement, which led to a brunch reception for friends and family six months after their elopement, exactly a year to the date they met. "We like to do things in six-month increments," she jokes.

The only reason they ended up in Vegas after just six months of dating was because Ben, who is from England, had always wanted to visit the city after seeing it in a movie as a child. En route to Vegas from LA, they stopped at the "World Famous Gold & Silver Pawn Shop," home of the ridiculously popular reality TV show *Pawn Stars*. Ben's mom is a huge fan, so they took some photos for her and had a look around, tried on some rings, joked about marriage, and left.

Once at their hotel, Treasure Island, the topic of marriage came up again, but for real this time. The more they talked about it, the more it made sense: Both were in their thirties, had done the dating scene, had good chemistry, and had similar views on life. There in the enormous bathroom of their Treasure Island hotel room, Ben got down on one knee and said, "Let's do it. Let's get married."

"Had I known we'd be getting married, we would have sprung for something much nicer," says Lana. "But it was kind of fun to stay at a slightly dilapidated pirate hotel. It sort of fit the mood of the weekend pretty well."

After ten minutes spent googling how to get married in Las Vegas, they set an alarm for 7:30 a.m. so they could be first in line at the Marriage License Bureau. After that was taken care of, they went back to the pawn shop and bought the rings: hers, a thin gold band holding a center diamond surrounded by six diamonds in the shape of a flower; his, a stainless steel wedding band. Now they just needed somewhere to actually *get* married, and also get their rental car back in time.

They ended up at A Little White Wedding Chapel, "getting married at the drive-through, in our rental Toyota Corolla, by a guy named Reverend Love—and he swore that that's his real name—leaning out of a window," says Lana. "It looked like we should be getting a McDonald's hamburger." (They got their rental back in time.)

However, when they returned home, she felt that something was missing—the community of marriage, the validation from family and friends. "I needed people to just see us, even though I didn't want the dress, and didn't want to spend $30,000 on some fancy dinner. It was kind of important for me to feel like other people were celebrating the fact that we'd found each other, especially at thirty-six and thirty-four."

So, on their six-month elopement anniversary (and, if you're following, their one-year anniversary of meeting), they threw an "elegant-casual" brunch for sixty-five guests in a historic ballroom in downtown DC. Ben's mother came from England, other family came from Seattle and LA and Atlanta, and friends came from Michigan and New York.

Lana's mother sponsored a caviar station and bought the cake. Lana considers her mother to be a traditional person, and says she was crushed that she didn't get to witness the vows. "She'd also spent all this time thinking about what it might be like to give me away, and to make a toast, all these sorts of traditional things. I found the one thing I guess she and I were both excited about, this cake thing. She threw herself into it, scheduling seven different tastings. And it turned out to be really wonderful. It bonded us, and I hope that she was happy with how everything turned out."

Ben and Lana also flew in one of her good friends from California to take formal wedding photos with their moms at sites around DC. "I think that made them feel really special, like we were acknowledging that they were a really important part of our lives," says Lana. "The cake was a nice bonding experience for me and my mom, but I think the pictures made [both moms] really feel like they were part of a story.

"It was so nice to just have this casual celebration, this validation, while also having this really private, intimate, perfect ceremony, that looking back on, I love that my hair wasn't washed, and we have these super terrible selfies, while also having these gorgeous professional pictures from our reception. The two together, I think, define us as a couple."

Lana & Ben's Fine Print

LIVE: Washington, DC

WORK: Lana is vice president of a financial company, and Ben is an electrician.

AGES WHEN THEY ELOPED: Lana was thirty-six and Ben was thirty-four.

RELATIONSHIP TIME LINE: Dated for six months → Engaged for one day → Eloped April 27, 2019 → Honeymooned April 28, 2019

PROPOSAL: Ben proposed in their Treasure Island hotel room.

WEDDING VENUE: "The World Famous Drive Thru Tunnel of Love Ceremony" at A Little White Wedding Chapel

VOWS: Neither remembers what they said—they just repeated after Rev Love.

DISTANCE FROM HOME TO VENUE: 2,424 miles / 3,901 km

NUMBER OF GUESTS: 0

SHE WORE: A white shirt and jeans

HE WORE: A white shirt and blue khakis

RINGS: Lana's ring is a thin gold band holding a center diamond with six diamonds around it in the shape of a flower. Ben's is a stainless steel wedding band.

SPENT: $150

HONEYMOON: The day after their drive-through elopement, they went to a day party at Encore Beach Club, which they consider to be their honeymoon.

PRO TIP: "If you're going to get married at the drive-through, spring for the convertible!"

Why You Should Elope in Las Vegas

Out of the more than forty million people who visit Las Vegas each year, a decent chunk head there solely to elope. There are ample opportunities for stunning elopements at any one of the area's many hotels, as well as at its iconic chapels.

Beyond the legendary "Welcome to Fabulous Las Vegas Nevada" sign and the Strip's dozens of hotels with their own tiers of elopement packages, you'll also find an abundance of protected natural zones in nearby corners of the Mojave Desert with insane backdrops for photo ops—did you know Nevada has more mountain ranges than any other state? And because we (and pretty much everyone else) have thrown that whole "What happens in Vegas…" rule out the window, why not bring some friends and loved ones along for the ride?

Good to Know

There's only one place you can get a marriage license in Las Vegas: The Marriage License Bureau inside the Clark County Clerk's Office in downtown Las Vegas. It's highly recommended that you fill out the pre-application online in order to avoid waiting in long lines or getting up at the ungodly-hour-for-Vegas time of 7:30 a.m. In most cases, the only documentation required as part of the application process is a government-issued ID (e.g., a passport or driver's license) from both parties. The courthouse is open every day (including holidays), 8 a.m. to midnight, and there's no waiting period, meaning you can marry as soon as you receive your marriage license (which should be a given), which expires after one year.

Note that your officiant must have a Certificate of Permission to Perform Marriages in the state of Nevada in order for your union to be legally

THE DAWN OF VEGAS ELOPEMENTS

Couples started eloping to Vegas in the 1930s, when the Strip was just a desolate, dusty road. The Great Depression had swallowed the country, and in order to stimulate the economy and grow Vegas's population of 5,165, Nevada governor Fred B. Balzar legalized gambling, which brought in gamblers from all over the country. He also plunked a marriage license bureau in the train depot and kept the county clerk's office open twenty-four hours a day, laying the foundation for quickie Vegas elopements as we now know them.

recognized. Most venues, including chapels, use only authorized officiants, so this typically isn't an issue—but for peace of mind, it's worth double-checking that yours is listed in the Nevada statewide database before planning your ceremony.

Las Vegas hosts around three hundred weddings a day. The most popular date? Valentine's Day.

WHEN TO GO:

September through November and January through February. For tolerant heat lovers, the hot but not I-want-to-die hot temps in the fall make it a great time of year to elope to Vegas—as does the dip in tourists. Skip December, unless you enjoy the spirited rush of a very, very crowded Strip and buffets that double in price. After New Year's and through February, though, things quiet down, and the temps settle in the 60s [16°C–21°C].

The spring, while warmer, can be quite windy, making outdoor portraits more difficult to capture. It's also full of special events— NASCAR weekend!—which attract mega crowds. Whatever you do, avoid heading there in summer—unless you're in favor of over 100°F [38°C] highs and very crowded pools.

If venturing on a truly last-minute elopement, seasons be damned, just be sure to first check the Las Vegas tourism board's convention schedule, which gives details on events across area hotels, so you can steer clear of surging room rates and determine where there might be no rooms at all.

PRO TIP:

If you have flexibility, or if you're taking some extra time off surrounding your elopement, consider a weekday ceremony. Since Vegas is a highly popular spot for weekend getaways, you'll find cheaper lodging and greater availability of vendors, venues, and restaurant reservations during the week (particularly Tuesday through Thursday).

Where to Elope in Vegas

While Las Vegas's chapels will always be a quick and easy go-to, you can now find options just off the Strip, so if your vibe is a little more cactus than Elvis, you're in luck. Here's what to know before you (spontaneously) go.

Chapels

GRACELAND WEDDING CHAPEL

The name says it all: This is the spot to go to if an Elvis ceremony is part of your big-day vision. Yes, you can find Elvises at many other Vegas chapels, but as the folks at this long-standing institution are dying to remind you, Graceland Wedding Chapel is widely recognized as the first place to conduct an Elvis ceremony, in 1977. The most basic of the Elvis packages includes photography, rose boutonnières, and a copy of Elvis and Priscilla's marriage certificate. (We'll just let that last bit sit there for a moment.)

Five other pricier options tack on extras such as livestreaming, videography, and floral bouquets, with the Famous Dueling Elvis Package marking the top-tier experience. It involves not one, but two impersonators bringing the action: Elvis in his early years, donning a gold lamé suit, and the King at his peak, outfitted in a sequin jumpsuit.

Most of the white chapels and other venues typically associated with Sin City elopements aren't actually located right on the Strip—they're a few blocks north, conveniently close to the Clark County Clerk's Office.

LITTLE CHURCH OF THE WEST

When it opened in 1942, the Little Church of the West was the first freestanding building in Vegas built to serve exclusively as a wedding chapel. Today, it's the only building on the Strip listed in the National Register of Historic Places, and as a result, retains much of its original look: cedar exterior, California redwood interior, and Victorian-era railroad-car lamps lighting the chapel. It offers elopements and weddings ranging from the pared-down "Let's Elope" package (you get a photographer, single rose and boutonnière, and certificate holder) to the "All Inclusive VIP" deal, which ramps things up a notch to include additional portraits, video options, florals, Champagne toasts, and a limo. There are western-themed elopement options too—cowboy boots encouraged—complete with a burlap-and-lace aisle runner.

SURE THING CHAPEL

The newest chapel in the city, but with an eclectic, old-school vibe (think Polaroid prints and a vintage record player), this spot is a charming alternative to the classic Strip venues. Started by three friends in the industry—the owner of a pop-up elopement business called Flora Pop, a photographer, and an officiant—Sure Thing Chapel is located on the casino-lined and neon-filled Fremont Street in Old Las Vegas. The venue allows you to BYOP (bring your own photographer), and many of its packages include the minister fee, marriage license filing fee, a bouquet and boutonnière, and yes, Polaroids.

Call it a micro wedding for the times. In 1967, Elvis Presley took off from Palm Springs in the middle of the night with his fiancée, Priscilla, on Frank Sinatra's borrowed private jet. Their destination? Las Vegas, naturally. At 10 a.m. on May 1, 1967, they married in a candle-filled suite at the Aladdin Hotel in front of fourteen close friends and family, which was immediately followed by a press conference, then a Champagne breakfast reception at the hotel (which is absolutely genius).

Desert

ELDORADO VALLEY DRY LAKE BED

This vast, flat expanse of cracked white-salt earth 30 miles [48 km] south of the Strip in Boulder City makes for a beautifully minimalist venue, framed at the horizon by distant mountains. Because of the sheer flatness and barrenness of Eldorado, it's also well suited for drone photography and videography, as well as neon-colored smoke bombs, which look phenomenal in photos against the blank landscape. Note that you do need a permit, which many local elopement planners have obtained.

RED ROCK CANYON NATIONAL CONSERVATION AREA

Just 16 miles [26 km] from Vegas, Red Rock Canyon National Conservation Area has become a popular option for those looking to marry in a natural environment without straying too far from the Strip. Sitting on a nearly 200,000-acre swath of the Mojave Desert, Red Rock Canyon is protected by the Bureau of Land Management for the preservation of its incredible geologic features—miles and miles of Aztec sandstone formations streaked with hues of red, orange, and brown, which make for captivating backdrops.

Several elopement companies in the area have obtained commercial permits to perform wedding services at Red Rock Canyon (and many include round-trip limo transportation in their packages). If you choose not to go through one of those services, you'll have to apply for a Special Recreation Permit, which comes with a fee that varies based on the size of your group and the number of paid vendors involved.

VALLEY OF FIRE

Nevada's oldest state park, this breathtaking, 40,000-acre span is marked by similar brick-red sandstone as Red Rock Canyon. Shifting sand dunes in the Jurassic period created the curved formations and an intense, burnt sienna palette. To hold your ceremony here, you'll need to go through a vendor that's been issued an exclusive Valley of Fire State Park permit, such as Cactus Collective Weddings. (This particular park does not allow individual vendors to receive the required permit for weddings on a one-off basis.)

Want to get married in a museum? Home to an incredible collection of neon signs plucked from now-defunct Vegas businesses dating back to the 1930s, Vegas's Neon Museum allows you to get married in its side lot, aptly dubbed the Neon Boneyard, where more than one hundred fifty relics of a bygone era have come to rest.

CHAPTER 6:

The Pos
Elopem
Party ar
Exchan

Tripp & Julie

Fresh off a morning of snowboarding at Wisp Resort in Maryland, Tripp and Julie decided they were going to elope. They were having lunch with friends in the lodge, and after listening to them complain about their wedding plans for quite some time, Julie looked at Tripp and said, "When we do this, do you just want to elope?"

It was only appropriate, then, to follow a ski resort proposal with ski resort nuptials. In January 2017, they eloped to Big Sky, Montana, where Tripp once taught snowboarding lessons and where they'd visited a couple of times while dating.

After signing their marriage license in front of the grand fireplace in one of the resort's hotel lobbies, they grabbed their snowboards and headed up the mountain with their officiant and photographer, both locals they had found online; Tripp's buddy Tom, who filmed the ceremony; and a random friend of Tom's who agreed to be the ring bearer.

Once at the top of the mountain, they followed a trail to a secluded spot, said their vows with Lone Mountain looming in the background, then zigzagged down as their photographer trailed them on skis. When they reached the bottom, says Tripp, "There were so many strangers taking pictures of us and congratulating us that we felt like celebrities."

Then they drove to another trail, hiked 1 mile [1.6 km] in 3 feet [91 cm] of snow—still in their formal attire—and posed for photos by a frozen waterfall. Afterward, they headed down to basecamp for their first meal as husband and wife: chili dogs.

Their photos ended up playing a key role in how Tripp and Julie broke the news to their parents. First, they told Julie's family during a gathering at her parents' home in DC. Pretending they were handing out belated Christmas gifts, Tripp and Julie gave everyone a framed photo from their elopement with their anniversary date printed on it, thinking this would be a clever way to announce the news. Instead, everyone wondered why Tripp and Julie were giving out pictures of themselves as gifts.

So they took out their rings. Still, nothing. Julie then announced: "Tripp and I got married in Montana. It's official." After yet another moment of "Huh?" it finally clicked, and the news was warmly received with hugs and tears.

A couple weeks later, Tripp's family gathered to celebrate his birthday at his parents' home in Richmond, Virginia. Using the same reveal method, he handed a photo collage to his mom, who screamed, "You got married?" The news was again well received, with more hugs and tears.

Later, both Tripp and Julie's families said that not only was the elopement smart and financially savvy, but it was also "so them," and they couldn't imagine Tripp and Julie having done it any other way.

However, both sides of the family urged Tripp and Julie to do something to celebrate their marriage. Nine months after their elopement, they held a cookout in a local park so friends and family members could join together and celebrate their marriage. Tripp and Julie bought the beer and wine, a local barbecue pig roaster provided most of the food, and a handful of guests brought homemade desserts.

While planning the celebration, Tripp and Julie asked their neighbor, Norm, who is an ordained minister, to speak, "so that everyone would feel connected to us in a 'wedding-esque' kind of way, instead of it just being a cookout," says Tripp. They met with Norm multiple times before the celebration, during which he asked them many of the same questions he asks an engaged couple before marriage: What are your expectations of each other? Why do you want to get married to each other? What are your thoughts on love?

Just before everyone sat down to eat, Norm stood before the guests with Julie and Tripp at his side and spoke. He shared their answers to his questions, along with more personal anecdotes, such as the significance of Julie's ring, stories about their elopement, the journey they took to get to know each other, and some wisdom from Dr. Seuss.

What advice does Tripp have for others who want to plan a celebration after their elopement? "Keep in mind why you eloped in the first place, and keep focused on those reasons so that the following ceremony doesn't spin out of control and you end up stressed out and tens of thousands of dollars in debt."

And, when planning the celebration, don't let on that it has anything to do with a wedding, or you'll get hit with the 30 percent wedding tax—they told park officials they were throwing a family reunion.

MARRIAGE ADVICE FROM NEIGHBOR NORM

Here are some sweet, hopeful sentiments that Norm shared during Tripp and Julie's party, applicable to love stories everywhere.

"You meet thousands of people, and none of them really touch you. And then you meet one person and your life changes forever for the better. Julie and Tripp, here are a few words of wisdom for a lasting and fulfilling marriage: No matter how busy you are, make time for yourselves. Hold hands. Unwind. Surprise each other. Find little chances every day to show you're grateful to be married. Julie, a word of advice about Tripp: The best way to get him to do something is to suggest that perhaps he is too old to do it. Always remember one of the most amazing gifts in life is to find someone who knows all your flaws, differences, and mistakes, yet still loves everything about you. Love one another and you will be happy. It's as simple and as difficult as that. In closing, I remind you two both of these words [inspired by] Dr. Seuss: I am excited to think of the places we will go and the adventures we will have along the way . . ."

Tripp & Julie's Fine Print

LIVE: Frederick, Maryland

WORK: Tripp is an administrator with the National Institutes of Health and a snowboard and ski instructor. Julie is a program manager at a biotechnology company.

AGES WHEN THEY ELOPED: He was thirty-four, and she was thirty.

TRIPP'S FIRST IMPRESSION: "I thought Julie was the complete package: smart, confident, responsible, sexy, and on time."

JULIE'S FIRST IMPRESSION: "He had very pretty eyes and was cute, honest, and had very interesting and unique experiences, having just returned from Ukraine for two years with the Peace Corps."

RELATIONSHIP TIME LINE: Dated for eighteen months → Engaged for around six months → Eloped January 2017 → BBQ celebration September 2017

WEDDING VENUE: Big Sky Resort, Montana

DISTANCE FROM HOME TO VENUE: 2,046 miles / 3,293 km

NUMBER OF GUESTS: Zero, just their officiant, photographer, Tripp's buddy Tom, who was also the videographer, and Tom's ring bearer friend

SHE WORE: A red bridesmaid's dress from the White by Vera Wang Collection from David's Bridal and a white faux fur cape

HE WORE: A tailored suit he'd bought in Thailand with a red tie to match Julie's dress

SOMETHING OLD AND BLUE: The diamonds in Julie's engagement ring belonged to Tripp's grandmother; the first-layer pants Julie wore under her dress were blue.

VOWS: Says Tripp: "I used lyrics from multiple songs to express how much I love Julie and look forward to building a life

together with her. Julie wrote some vows about how much I mean to her and added some funny stories about events in our lives together that proved to her how well suited we are."

RINGS: Tripp took one large diamond from his grandmother's ring and added multiple small diamonds to create a new ring for Julie. Since red is her favorite color, he also added small rubies. She's "tough on jewelry," so the band is platinum. For his ring, he went with a Tungsten band with a dark red dinosaur fossil inlay and a small, single diamond. "I wanted the Tungsten for its

weight and strength. The fossil was cool, and the colors varied based on the minerals in the earth where [the dinosaur] was found. And since men's wedding bands don't normally have a diamond and that was an option, I went for it."

SPENT: $5,672

BIGGEST SPLURGE: The entire weeklong trip, which was also their mini-moon. As wedding gifts to each other, Julie bought Tripp a spa visit, and he bought her private snowboarding lessons.

Why You Should Have a Post-Elopement Party

As eloping has evolved to encompass the many versions described in this book, so have the ways couples choose to celebrate with, and announce their news to, loved ones. Involving your family members in this momentous life event in some capacity will go a long way, especially for those families who are more traditional. A post-elopement party is the perfect way to do that.

Maybe you sit with your mom and design a menu for a backyard brunch. You let your dad walk you down the aisle, whatever that may look like. Does your brother want to give a speech? Let him.

Also—and more importantly—if you live far away from your family, a post-elopement celebration gives both sides a reason to come together and meet for the first time, and in a far less intense setting than a wedding (or even an engagement party).

Just remember—if it's your parents who are pushing for the post-elopement party, there's a good chance they'll pay for it, as Tripp and Julie's did. But if you feel overwhelmed at any point by the planning, you're entitled to walk away or reschedule—there really are no rules for any of this (and if there were, you already broke them).

When to Have a Post-Elopement Party

The big picture: It's good form not to wait *too* long to throw your post-elopement ceremony. Most couples wait six months, and some go for the tidiness of the one-year mark. Try not to wait much longer than that unless there's a good reason to do so (e.g., a deployment, pregnancy, or illness).

The little picture: If you're planning on throwing your bash at a venue or hiring any vendors, don't compete with wedding season.

Who to Invite

Who did you send physical announcements to, or personally call, to share the news of your marriage? Invite them to your post-elopement bash.

What to Emphasize

Food and alcohol. Forget the other trappings of a wedding—the dress, the hair, the makeup.

> What about gifts? Don't expect them (or worse, ask), but if you're being pestered by loved ones about what to get you, take an hour and create a registry.

Incorporating Traditions and Rituals

By following your elopement with a celebration that includes both families, you create a relaxed setting for both sides to bring together their different religions and traditions. This can be done with food, traditional clothing, dancing, music, readings, or any other meaningful elements.

Vow Renewals

A vow renewal is sort of like shouting through a megaphone and saying, "Hey, world! We got married in case you forgot!" You're basically making it known that you married this person, and you're ready to do it all over again.

While vow renewals are often associated with landmark anniversaries, there are other reasons to have one too. Some couples who eloped or had a bare-bones wedding might choose to renew their vows when they can afford to do something grander. For others, it might symbolize moving on from a rough patch in their marriage. And don't feel like you have to recite the same, deeply personal vows you said when you eloped; many couples opt to exchange a set of scripted, less personal vows in front of their family and friends.

Or, if you're looking to add a dose of romance after many years, you're free to head overseas and renew your vows wherever the heck you'd like—there are no laws around vow renewals in most countries. So go ahead, put on your wedding garb and shout your vows from a gondola in Venice if you damn well please. Just bring your paperwork with you as backup.

CHAPTER 7:

The Cou Ceremo

rthouse

ny

Elizabeth & RJ

The day RJ proposed to Elizabeth, they had gone to a Christmas tree farm and chopped down their tree. That night, after they'd finished decorating it, he proposed with a ring he'd bought several months before and had hid in their new apartment in Savannah, Georgia. "It wasn't grand or showboat-y," says Elizabeth. "It was real. We knew that some big things were coming our way." It was just after 9/11, and RJ was a member of the US Army.

They consider themselves traditional and had been planning to get married in a church wedding in November 2002, knowing that his unit would be deployed soon after (they didn't even attempt to plan a honeymoon). Then, one day the following summer, "RJ came home with a very serious look on his face and said we needed to talk," says Elizabeth. He had learned that he was being sent to the Middle East early for an assignment and there was no guarantee that he was going to be home in time for their wedding. "I remember him suggesting that we should look into a

justice of the peace (JOP) wedding as early as that week. I didn't take him seriously."

As they talked it through, though, they both realized it was the right decision. "I remember us having some very serious conversations about what was to come and how we needed to support each other through these big things. Marriage is hard, but add these stressors—war, long times away from each other, fear—and you need to be sure that you are in the right head-space to commit to that."

A few days later, on a Tuesday in early August, they took their lunch breaks and headed to the Chatham County Courthouse in Savannah. They drove separately and wore their work clothes, she in a business suit and he in his flight uniform. Elizabeth was a reporter at the time, and her boss at the news station called Superior Court Judge Ronald Ginsberg and explained their situation. Could he squeeze them in? Of course.

The ceremony took ten minutes. Elizabeth's favorite memory was seeing RJ run into the courthouse in his "pickle suit" (flight suit). Afterward, they celebrated with lunch at a nearby sandwich spot. Her only regret is that they didn't take any photos—she forgot to bring her camera, and their cell phones didn't double as cameras like they do today.

Looking back, "I never questioned it," says RJ. "I knew this was the best thing because I wanted Elizabeth to get the support from my Army family that I knew she would need while I was gone."

As Elizabeth got to know more couples in the military, she realized that JOP weddings are not at all uncommon. "I feel like part of a club now that we have a JOP anniversary and a church wedding anniversary. So many military families have similar stories."

What would she tell other couples in the same situation? "It's really not about the ceremony at all. It's about you and that person and the life you are about to start together. Don't get too caught up in all the details."

Elizabeth & RJ's Fine Print

LIVE: Oahu, Hawaii

WORK: Elizabeth is a program manager for a nonprofit and RJ is an officer in the US Army.

AGES WHEN THEY ELOPED: She was twenty-five, and he was twenty-eight.

ELIZABETH'S FIRST IMPRESSION: "He was well-dressed, sweet, and very chivalrous—a gentleman. I actually remember when we were walking down the street to one of the bars, there was a lot of traffic and cars on the road, and RJ asked me if we could switch places, as I was walking closest to the road. I remember thinking that was a very gentlemanly thing to do."

RJ'S FIRST IMPRESSION: "She was down-to-earth and beautiful."

RELATIONSHIP TIME LINE: Dated for one year → Engaged November 2001 → Eloped August 2002 → Honeymooned 2006

WEDDING VENUE: Chatham County Courthouse in Savannah, Georgia.

DISTANCE FROM HOME TO VENUE: 15.7 miles / 25 km

NUMBER OF GUESTS: 0

SHE WORE: A business suit

HE WORE: His flight uniform

RING: A classic one-carat round-cut diamond

SPENT: $50

PRO TIP: "Be flexible and adaptable. I never in a million years thought that I would have a JOP wedding before my actual wedding. Military life definitely threw us a curveball, and I'm glad I didn't get all worked up and upset about it. It definitely prepared me for military life in general and what to expect."

Why You Should Elope at a Courthouse

It's fast.

It's easy.

It's cheap.

Since you're heading straight to the source, you'll have total peace of mind that all of your paperwork is legit.

It requires very little planning.

The Courthouse Checklist

Brush up on the specifics of your courthouse before you arrive. This seems obvious, but many couples assume you can just show up and get married. Here's what to look for when (lightly) planning.

- Figure out whether you can apply online. If you must apply in person, you will likely need to make an appointment.

- For states that require appointments for the ceremony, there are, in some cases, months-long wait lists. Other states don't allow appointments at all, and you show up only to wait hours for your turn. Be armed with this information before making concrete plans that might include inviting guests.

- Note that most civil ceremony appointments are on weekday mornings or early afternoons.

- Know that you're only going to get around ten minutes.

- Determine whether you're allowed to read your own vows—usually, this isn't the case, but there are exceptions. Sometimes a judge or clerk will allow you to say something personal to one another after he or she has finished the standard script.

MILITARY ELOPEMENTS

For some couples, like Elizabeth and RJ, going the courthouse route is done out of pure necessity due to unique military situations and the unknown factors that come with that, like sudden deployment to a war zone.

Quick military weddings first became common during World War II. In 1942, two-thirds of weddings were brides marrying men newly enlisted in the military. A *Vogue* article at the time stated, "The 1942 schedule may run something like this: engagement announcement on Monday, invitations sent out by telegraph on Wednesday, the last handful of rice and rose petals flung on Saturday." Many couples eloped during periods of leave (short trips home), taking trains to Reno or Las Vegas to tie the knot. And many were married once the soldier returned home for good, the brides wearing modest dresses made of silk from the parachutes that had saved their grooms in battle.

Today, military JOP weddings are likely to happen before a soldier heads off to war, or once they're home for good, rather than during a deployment. For situations involving rapid deployment, some states will nix the waiting period. In Texas, for example, the seventy-two-hour waiting period is automatically waived if a soldier is considered active duty.

- Most—but not all—courthouses allow indoor photography. Before you get your heart set on photos, double-check this to be sure.

- Some courthouses have obscure rules for seemingly no reason. For instance, until 2018, Richmond's courthouse banned cell phones. Now, they lock them in a cabinet when you arrive. Sniff out any fuzzy rules ahead of time if you can.

The Five Best-Looking City Halls

Just because you're going the civil route doesn't mean it has to be ordinary. The United States has a slew of gorgeous courthouses, each with its own set of cool trivia and optimal photo ops. Here are our top picks for doing city hall in style.

Boston

Built in 1968 in the Brutalist architecture style—which is the sophisticated way of saying "heavy on the concrete"—Boston City Hall has taken a lot of heat over the years from those with untrained eyes. But thanks to 1980s fashion photographers who discovered that concrete "photographs well," as it provides a neutral background that complements skin tones, your courthouse ceremony shots will have you basically looking like a model.

Pittsburgh

Simply put, the Allegheny County Courthouse in downtown Pittsburgh is completely badass. The Romanesque Revival structure features soaring Syrian arches and French Gothic dormer windows (plus a tower!) and has been named the second-best courthouse in America by the American Institute of Architects (not bad, considering the number one spot goes to the US Supreme Court Building). Say your vows indoors at the top of the sweeping Grand Staircase, or head to the romantic courtyard in the building's center.

San Francisco

If there's one thing San Francisco is infamous for, it's being *not cheap*. But if you have your heart set on eloping there, not to worry, as it's got one of the most phenomenal courthouses in the country. The Beaux Arts building offers myriad spaces for ceremonies both indoors and out, but the main event is its marble and sandstone Grand Staircase that leads to the sun-drenched Ceremonial Rotunda on the second floor.

> If you're opting for a "destination courthouse" elopement in the United States, remember that the state in which you apply for your marriage license does not need to be the state where you currently reside. You do, however, need to get married in the state where you apply—marriage licenses don't transfer from state to state, meaning you can't apply for one in Montana and then head on down to Wyoming to get legally married. Just be sure to have the required forms of ID and money for any fees with you upon arrival at the courthouse, as outlined in chapter 1.

Santa Barbara

Attention, lovers of white-washed stucco, clay tile roofs, and bell towers: We present to you the Santa Barbara County Courthouse, home to all three of those charming features. Finished in 1929, the Spanish Colonial Revival building is hugely popular for elopements thanks to its six famous gardens reserved for ceremonies of fifteen people or fewer (you can elope in the bell tower too).

Seattle

Have you ever heard the words "rooftop" and "venue" and "free" used in the same sentence? No? Well, say hello to the Seattle Municipal Courthouse. On top of the building's twenty-three stories is an observation deck where ceremonies are performed year-round for free, rain or shine, even at night. Bring a group or just yourselves—and don't forget your umbrella.

> We wanted to root for you, Chicago, we really did. But your city hall's lush, rooftop greenspace (open for scheduled tours, not ceremonies) and Neoclassical-inspired interior does little to soften the fact that your wedding ceremonies are performed in a small, windowless room in the basement. Maybe next century.

HISTORY IS (FINALLY) MADE

On June 26, 2015, in a long-sought victory for gay rights, the US Supreme Court ruled that same-sex couples could marry nationwide. For the first time in history, legally married gay couples would receive the same benefits under federal law as other married couples, even if they lived in one of the states that did not, at the time, recognize same-sex marriage.

As revelers flooded the streets in cities across the country, many gay couples rushed to the courthouse to become the first same-sex marriages to take place in their states. In Texas, some judges waived the seventy-two-hour waiting period to allow these couples to marry right away; in Dallas, George Harris, eighty-two at the time, and Jack Evans, eighty-five, became the first gay couple to be issued a marriage license and were married after fifty-four years as a couple. Courthouses in Alabama that had upheld the state's Supreme Court decision to halt issuance of same-sex marriage licenses that spring reversed this decision and opened their doors to gay couples.

In Washington, DC, hundreds took to the steps of the US Supreme Court to celebrate, waving flags and rejoicing, while inside some lawmakers were emotional, dabbing their eyes out of joy. One of them, the late, great Ruth Bader Ginsburg, had been the driving force behind the ruling. In 2013, she became the first Supreme Court Justice to officiate a same-sex wedding (same-sex marriage was legalized in DC in 2010). "I think it will be one more statement that people who love each other and want to live together should be able to enjoy the blessings and the strife in the marriage relationship," she said at the time.

It is thanks in part to Ginsburg's trailblazing efforts as a Supreme Court Justice that gay marriage was legalized nationwide two years later. She died in 2020, but her trailblazing legacy and advocacy for LGBTQ+ rights endure.

Make It Your Own

While there are many things you can't do in a courthouse ceremony—celebratory tequila shots, a bouquet toss, the "Cupid Shuffle"—the experience is still yours to personalize in other ways. Have fun with your attire, throw in some florals that won't get tossed, and properly treat yourselves after you're legally wed.

Attire

The aesthetic of the courthouse room in which you say your vows is likely to be a bit, shall we say, *subdued*. This creates a host of options to have fun with your attire. Wear a jumpsuit or a sequin minidress. Pair a tulle skirt with a simple camisole, or try a tailored suit or *le smoking*, a woman's tuxedo (see page 59). Some designers have even devoted entire collections to civil ceremony dresses, such as Laure de Sagazan, whose delicate white dresses made of crepe, lace, and silk are definitely to be worn again. BHLDN's "City Hall" collection includes sharp, fitted pantsuits in black or white and flirty tea-length dresses.

If opting for a veil, you might consider a pillbox hat with a small piece of netting attached (called a fascinator in the fashion world).

Or go with what is known as a birdcage-style veil, a sassy piece made of French net that drops only in the front, hitting just below the nose. If your vision includes something closer to floor length, that's a go too.

> You're not going to find any dressing rooms in a courthouse, so do your hair and makeup at home (or in the car en route) and arrive dressed for the occasion. Or, the public restroom is always an option, if you don't mind an audience.

Floral Ideas

Chill day, chill bouquet. If you decide to have flowers, go for simple and sweet varieties, which also happen to ring up cheaply and come with *quite* apt meanings.

- Carnations: Love; white carnations symbolize *pure* love
- Daisies: New beginnings and cheerfulness
- Peonies: Romance and a happy marriage
- Red tulips: Perfect love
- Sunflowers: Adoration and loyalty

After the Courthouse, It's the After-Party

To properly cement the occasion, think about throwing an after-party, something simple and fun to match the pressure-free vibe of the day.

- Gather your loved ones for brunch at your favorite restaurant.
- Order takeout and have a picnic in a nearby park.
- Hit your favorite dive bar and partake in all the free shots.
- Throw a backyard barbecue for friends and family.
- Take that money you saved and splurge on a spa day.
- Or just head straight for your honeymoon.

CHAPTER 8

The Intimate

Dinner Party

Herbie & Chris

When it came to planning their wedding in Philadelphia, Herbie and Chris started with what they *didn't* want: First, they knew they didn't want a big wedding. They also didn't want to get married at city hall. They briefly considered having it in the park across the street from their apartment, but the urban setting meant too many people and unwanted noise.

They decided on a small, intimate ceremony followed by a big party later where everyone was invited. But as they began planning, the "small" ceremony started inching its way into a party, until it turned into what felt like the big, high-stress wedding they were avoiding in the first place. "It got to the point where we pumped the brakes on every-thing," says Chris. "We were like, why are we doing this? We should just do our own thing."

So they did. Through an online magazine, they found Vaux Studio, an intimate ceremony space in Center City. Because Vaux's capacity was capped at twenty-four people total due to its fire code, they next had to determine their pared-down guest list and what "level" of family member they wanted to invite. This proved to be just as hard to do with a small count as a big one.

"It got to the point where we kind of had to put a hard stop to it, or else it'd get too out of control. If we invited one aunt, we'd have to invite another aunt," says Herbie. They ultimately decided that since they have "symmetrical" families—in that they each have two parents and a younger sister—that that was who they'd invite. Their good friend Josh would be their officiant, and that was it.

But what about dinner? "I love food, and I love cooking, and my longtime favorite thing to do is just to go out to eat and try new restaurants," says Herbie. "Food is an integral part of our relationship."

For the celebratory dinner, they started looking for private rooms at restaurants. But they couldn't go to a noisy restaurant, as Chris's father is hard of hearing. Herbie's mom is gluten-free and allergic to onions, his father and sister are "just a smidge picky," and Chris's mom and sister are both vegetarian.

Then, Herbie says, he had a "light bulb thought of a crazy idea." For their six-year anniversary, he had surprised Chris with an Italian cooking class in the home of Joe and Angela Cicala that he'd found on Airbnb Experiences—Joe's a James Beard–nominated chef and Angela's one of Philadelphia's most celebrated pastry chefs. They made gnocchi with Sunday gravy, garlic bread, and homemade wine, and afterward, Chris suggested they walk for a bit as they were completely stuffed. Then, in the middle of a random street in South Philly, he proposed.

When Herbie reached back out to Angela, he told her about their engagement story and asked— and this was the "light bulb thought of a crazy idea"—if they'd consider letting them do another cooking class, but as their reception, and with their families.

Angela instantly loved the idea. They held a call to hash out the menu details and came up with something that worked for everyone: eggplant involtini, meat and meatless meatballs, potato gnocchi, gluten-free pasta, cannolis, and homemade wine. Their wedding cake was a gluten-free carrot cake from a local cake shop.

The cooking class reception was their favorite part of the wedding day. "It spoke to who we are as a couple, and was a really fun, cooldown experience after an emotional ceremony," says Chris.

Chris & Herbie's Fine Print

LIVE: Philadelphia, Pennsylvania

WORK: Chris is a marketing manager, and Herbie is a graphic designer.

AGES WHEN THEY GOT MARRIED: They were both twenty-seven.

CHRIS'S FIRST IMPRESSION: "Herbie seemed like someone I should get to know from the moment I met him. He was funny, smart, and easy to talk to—and easy on the eyes."

HERBIE'S FIRST IMPRESSION: "Chris was nice, easy to talk to, and I wanted to find out more about him."

RELATIONSHIP TIME LINE: Dated for six years → Engaged for three months → Eloped October 2018 → Honeymooned November 2018

WEDDING VENUE: Vaux Studio

NUMBER OF GUESTS: 6

CHRIS WORE: Custom suit by Indochino

HERBIE WORE: ASOS wedding suit

RINGS: Their wedding bands are from a local shop in Philadelphia called Bario Neal that specializes in ethically sourced materials. They both got sterling silver bands in the same style with different widths.

SPENT: Their total was $3,638.52, but thanks to their parents chipping in to cover the venue, cooking class, and photographer, they ended up only paying around $900.

BIGGEST SPLURGE: Photographer. They wanted to have photos to look back on and also share with those who couldn't be there.

HONEYMOON: They took an already-booked trip to Paris, Barcelona, and London and turned it into their honeymoon.

WHAT THEY DID WITH THE MONEY THEY SAVED: Splurged on fancy dinners during their European honeymoon

Why You Should Have a Dinner Party Wedding

Few things in life are more joyful than the simple pleasure of bringing together those closest to you for delicious food, good drinks, and great conversation. Factor in the momentous occasion that's called getting married, and you've got a heady cocktail of pure bliss—for you and your selected guests, who are likely thrilled to celebrate you in this very relaxed, intimate environment instead of yet another huge blowout event. No one has to dance if they don't want to. There's no embarrassing garter toss to try and unsee.

Overall, having an intimate dinner party wedding is great because it allows you to rein in that pesky area that typically causes a mountain of wedding-planning stress when considering a grander scale: the guest list. A small guest list means you're saving money—on everything—and therefore ameliorating the biggest argument that percolates between partners when planning a large-scale wedding.

Whether you have a dinner party at home or at a restaurant, distillery, or dive bar, you'll save money simply because you have fewer mouths to feed, no expensive entertainment to provide, and only a smattering of paper invitations to pay for if you opt not to text or email. And if you do the former, you're looking at $3 to $8 a head for the entire "invitation suite"—save-the-dates, reception cards, menu cards, thank-you cards, and place cards—versus, on average, $600 to $800 in total for a hundred-person wedding—before postage. For perspective, your entire menu for an intimate gathering might only cost $600.

How to Pull It Off

Create the Guest List

With an intimate dinner party, you still have to face creating a guest list. However, when it's a super-small affair, it's often easier to be black-and-white about it. Start with immediate family (the ones you like) and your closest friends—those who are close enough that they'll be in your lives, in some capacity, pretty much forever.

Most restaurants consider "intimate" to be twenty-five to thirty guests. If you're hosting your dinner party in your home, you might want to trim that to ten to twelve—a number that can fit around a large table (any more than that and you'll run into multiple tables, which inevitably sucks for conversation). Overall, by keeping the guest count small, you guarantee you'll be surrounded only by the family members and close friends you really want to share this incredibly meaningful day with, a day that you'll look back on with fondness for its amber ambience and joyful mood, sort of like Friendsgiving.

Select the Location

A short guest list and smaller budget open up a bounty of options as far as venues go. This is generally a good thing, but don't let it get overwhelming; instead, start with settling on a location. Take a hard look at where your guests live. If many of them are elderly family members, and it's deeply important to you or your partner that they're there, you should probably give up your vision of an enchanting Napa dinner al fresco and aim instead for a place that's drivable for them—don't force anyone to get on a plane, especially if you're doing this with a few weeks' notice.

Or, if you're hell-bent on a location because it's extremely personal and significant to you as a couple, but it's expensive or a bit of an endeavor for your guests to get to (see enchanting Napa dinner), be realistic about who will actually show up, and don't begrudge those who can't attend.

Pick a Date

Your date will largely depend on when your venue is available. If it's one that usually accommodates large weddings, which is many venues' bread and butter, you'll have better luck aiming for the wedding off-season, which is typically November to March. If your date is inflexible because of work conflicts, or it's rushed due to a loved one's health, look into having your dinner party at home or at a restaurant that's able to accommodate your guest count with short notice, or can set you up during an off-hour slot, such as midafternoon on a weekday. (This advice gets tossed in December, when most restaurants are booked seven days a week with holiday parties.)

Hire Vendors

At minimum, you're going to want professional photographs, particularly if your setting is dim and candlelit. As is heavily advised in chapter 2, nab a great photographer well in advance, and consider splurging on having your hair and makeup professionally done.

Invite Your Guests

To paper or not to paper, that is the question. If you're the kind of couple who sends out a holiday card with a photo of yourselves and the dog, then paper might be your medium of choice. Consider sending out postcards, which are charming and will save you on paper and postage. Or call, text, or email your guests, which works just fine for loved ones who know you well and won't be miffed by the informality. Paperless Post offers a text option too (with GIFs!),

while its classic email invitations always jazz up an inbox.

Regardless of how you invite your guests, a nice bonus is that the small number keeps tracking RSVPs extremely manageable, even if it's just in a shared Google Doc with your partner.

Tell Your Guests What to Wear

When it comes to attending a party, nothing is more anxiety inducing than feeling like you might be underdressed. Do your guests a solid and let them know how relaxed or formal they should look, depending on the venue. Even if it's the chillest spot—your home—there's a good chance you and your partner will be gussied up, so let your guests know to dress accordingly if it's important to you (professional photos framed on the mantel come to mind).

Figure Out Transportation

Very often, the dinner party venue you select will be the site of both the ceremony and the reception, which makes just about everything—you guessed it—easier. If it's not—say you have a church ceremony followed by dinner in the next neighborhood over—shuttling your guests to the restaurant is a breeze with a handful of Ubers you can gracefully and discreetly arrange and pay for.

Give Thought to the Small Details

Place cards, a classic hallmark of any dinner party worth its salt, are a detail you shouldn't skip. You don't need to get all escort card intense, but simple, handwritten place cards are a basic courtesy to your guests. And since they're probably wondering where you're sitting, place cards prevent anyone from unwittingly taking your seats and sipping the Dom you had reserved for yourselves.

The Restaurant Dinner Party

Think about the best date you and your partner have ever been on. Now invite your parents. Kidding . . . sort of. Having an intimate dinner party ceremony at a place meaningful to you—whether it's your favorite brasserie where the servers have long known your names or a beloved rooftop bar with city views—is forever romantic. Even if it's the diner you went to every hungover Saturday when you first started dating (or last week).

It's also a pretty solid power move, if you can afford it (you will spend substantially more on the food versus doing it at home). But for some couples, pampering yourselves and your guests in a private room at a restaurant that's special to you is entirely worth it, especially when considering the lack of prep and cleanup involved. And unintended couch guests.

Food and Drinks

Very often, you can work with a restaurant's chef on creating a special menu and collaborate with the bar manager on a signature cocktail. But don't gloss over the bar's fine print—there are different rules at every establishment for buying out the bar, and you don't want to be knocked over the head with a massive bill at the end of the night. Be sure to clarify—in writing—what's expected when renting out any size space.

Dessert

Dessert—usually in the form of a wedding cake—is also something to discuss with restaurant managers. If you're permitted to bring in a cake from an outside baker, be prepared to pay a cutting fee. Or, if a freezer-burned piece of cake on your one-year anniversary is something you can give up, save money by serving one of the house's signature desserts.

Decorations

Behold, the tablescape. Or, rather, a subdued version of it. Check to see whether the restaurant will let you bring in your own floral centerpieces or runners—some will be cool with it, but some establishments have in-house florists (which sounds very late '90s SoHo but is, in fact, still a thing), so be sure to follow the rules.

Ask About Having a Dedicated Point Person

For any menu changes, ongoing decoration requests, or surprises (last-minute RSVPs), it's important to have a point person at the restaurant you can text and hear back from quickly. It's peace of mind for both parties involved.

The At-Home Dinner Party

Having a postnuptial dinner party at home offers a fair deal of flexibility: You get to create your own day-of time line (cocktail hour before the front porch ceremony? Sure!); incorporate sweet, sentimental touches like the family china; and really be in control of how much you spend on those notorious budget hogs: food and drinks. When the last guest is gone, or passed out on your couch, there's little more to do than turn off the lights and sink into bed. Here's what to tackle and when to do it.

Decide on the Menu

The very, *very* last thing you want to do on your wedding day is panic over whether the goat cheese–filled figs are burning. Do not attempt to do any part of the cooking yourself—there's a good chance you've never hosted this many people before (or this many courses, for that matter). Consider having the whole thing catered or hiring a private chef.

Or maybe you have a family member who offers to cook, or a highly reliable best friend who gifts you with a sweet spread from Costco. (No shame here—the food court pizza is absurdly good and can be ordered ahead for pickup, and the array of dips and cheese boards is always a good bet. Plus, the Kirkland wine is quite nice for store brand.) In these two instances, go ahead and make it family style, or have your reliable friend arrange a buffet on the kitchen island. Just whatever you do, stay out of the kitchen, unless it's to grab a second bottle of Champagne for getting-ready mimosas.

Embrace the Tablescape

You don't need to go full on with a perfectly cheesy theme here if you don't want to (you know, like your college colors), but you should create a tablescape because that's what elevates a regular Saturday night dinner party from one followed by Pictionary to one celebrating your marriage. First off, candles are a must. Keep floral centerpieces shallow enough that you can have a conversation across the table without having to shuffle them around (which still happens for no good reason this far into the twenty-first century). In fact, consider skipping florals altogether and go with a runner made out of just greenery. Your aunt will think its edgy, and you'll save a bunch of money.

Timing It

If a dinner party wedding à la maison sounds like you, here's a time line to guide the basics:

Six Months Out

- Research vendors and reach out for interviews. If it's a match, hire them as soon as you can, as if this were a "real" wedding.

- Determine whether you're entrusting the menu to a loved one, and if not, begin researching caterers or private chefs.

- Send around informal save-the-dates so your out-of-town guests can make travel arrangements.

Three Months Out

- Send out formal invitations and a list of nearby hotel or Airbnb accommodations. Try to determine who assumes they're staying with you.

- If you're going with a chef or caterer, sign contracts.

- Discuss menu options and decide whether you're going to provide the alcohol, or whether the chef or caterer is. Hint: You will save a lot of money if you buy it yourself.

One Month Out

- Firm up your guest count and continue to try to determine who's staying with you.

- Decide whether you need to rent tables, chairs, or linens.

- Take inventory of your glassware, plate, bowl, and silverware situation, and figure out what you need at each place setting, given the menu. (This is if you're not using a catering service, which should bring place settings and linens with them as part of the price point at which you hired them.)

One Week Out

- Confirm your guest count again; things happen at the last minute.

- Let the chef or caterer know immediately of any guest count changes. When a small number of guests shrinks or grows—even by one person— it can considerably affect the overall bill.

- If BYOBing, buy booze, mixers, and nonperishable garnishes.

- Stock up on reusable containers so you can send guests home with leftovers.

Day Before

- Buy ice. If this is an outdoor, warm-weather party, buy more than you think you'll need.

- Buy citrus garnishes and any herbs for cocktails, such as basil or mint.

- Clean. If you live in a metropolitan area, you can treat yourself to an on-demand cleaning crew through an app such as SendWork, which locates cleaners near you on hyper-short notice. They'll whiz in before the party for a spot clean or deep dive into the bathroom and also clean up afterward, either post–dinner party or the next morning. Bless technology.

- Set the table if you're not having it catered.

> On tipping: If your catering contract doesn't include gratuity, you should tip 15 to 20 percent of the total bill, or $50 to $100 for each chef. And don't forget the servers, who should at least get $20 to $50 each. Same goes for each member of the cleaning crew.

- Get married.
- Eat, drink, cry, and try not to lose your phone.

Day After

- Have breakfast drinks in bed.
- Look for your phone.

> Going super simple? Grab a case of Trader Joe's "Two-Buck Chuck," pour it into vases posing as carafes, and order Chinese to eat family style with your guests. No one can judge your taste because it's your day.

Day Of

- Have your most trustworthy friend pick up any flower arrangements and arrive two to three hours before the other guests to help create the perfectly relaxed tablescape.

- By now, your fridge is likely packed, so ask someone to bring an extra cooler or three.

- Have your extra-cooler person grab another bag of ice on the way. You always need more ice.

- Sip mimosas or whiskey or Coors Light and relax somewhere removed from the kitchen. Now would be a great time to write your vows if you've let those slide.

> Oversize ice cubes aren't just for the mixologists everyone loves to hate—big chunks of ice actually keep cocktails from getting watered down too quickly, so if you're serious about your old-fashioneds, consider investing in a couple of silicone trays.

THE BAR CART

Rather than use precious kitchen counter space (which will irk your hired chef), utilize a bar cart. Don't have one? A low bookshelf, small table, or even a vintage vanity will do. Once you've figured that out, here are the core essentials for creating a stocked, at-home bar.

Liquor: Vodka, tequila (white), rum (light), gin, bourbon, Scotch (blended), sweet and dry vermouth

Beer: Light, dark, IPAs

Cider: Dry and sweet

Wine: White, red, rosé

Bubbles: Champagne, prosecco, sparkling rosé

Mixers: Club soda, tonic water, sparkling water, ginger ale, Coca-Cola, orange juice, cranberry juice

Garnishes: Limes, lemons, green olives, maraschino cherries, kosher salt

Accessories: Corkscrew, bottle opener, paring knife, small cutting board, juice squeezer, standard shaker, jigger, cocktail napkins, toothpicks, swizzle sticks

Glasses: Martini, highball, wine, pint, Champagne

KNOW YOUR BUBBLES: FIVE DAY-OF PAIRINGS

There is one common denominator ubiquitous to celebrations the world over: Champagne. Historically associated with eighteenth-century European aristocracy as a status symbol among the courts, the bubbly then made its way to Napoleon's army, where *sabrage*, the act of opening a bottle with a ceremonial saber, is said to have originated, before eventually finding itself in championship locker room spray fests everywhere. Along the way, it became the drink of choice at wedding celebrations the world over.

   Here, Vanessa Price, sommelier and author of *Big Macs & Burgundy: Wine Pairings for the Real World*, shares her top recs for five moments during the day when bubbles are a must: getting ready, during toasts, eating cake, dancing into the night, and a special something for just the two of you to hide away and share during the festivities.

$ = less than $25

$$ = $25 to $75

$$$ = $75 to $200

$$$$ = $200 to $500

$$$$$ = $500+

1. **Gettin' Gussied: PÉTILLANT NATUREL**

   The ritual of getting ready on the big day is almost as sacred as the vows themselves. It's a time to spend those last few moments of single-dom with loved ones laughing, celebrating, and preparing for the lifetime commitment soon to come. It's also about cute getting-ready pics and a little buzz to kick off the festivities. Enter pét-nat, short for pétillant naturel, which translates to "natural sparkling" wine. Not only is pét-nat fresh, fruity, and delicious, but it also tends to be lower in alcohol than other sparklers (read: 10 a.m.–friendly). Plus, it comes in a rainbow of shades, from electric purple to sunshine yellow to deeply hued magenta, making for some truly Insta-worthy shots.

$$ Birichino Pétulant Naturel Malvasia Bianca, Monterey, California, USA

$$ La Garagista Farm + Winery "Grace & Favour" La Crescent, Vermont, USA

$$ Macari Family Vineyards "We're Not There to Fork Spiders" Cabernet Franc Rosé, North Fork, New York, USA

2. **A Toast to Please the Masses: DEUTSCHER SEKT**

   Selecting a crowd-pleasing sparkler can be challenging: You need something with enough elegance that your wine snob cousin who spent a year in Italy won't scoff, but basic enough that Uncle Ralph can enjoy it too. This is where German sparkling bruts come in, which is what you should choose for your celebratory cheers. They mainly comprise Riesling grapes, and the levels of dryness are similar to Champagne (brut still means dry here). Best of all, you can get top-quality stuff for less than $25 a bottle. When you see bottles of German fizz, look for labels that say "Deutscher Sekt bestimmter Anbaugebiete" or "Winzersekt." The former means it's a quality sparkling wine of distinction made in one of thirteen designated wine regions, so it didn't just come from anywhere. And the latter, Winzersekt, is *the* top designation; when you see it on a label it means the wine was estate-grown from only one kind of grape. Guarantee your cousin doesn't know *that*.

   $ Sektkellerei Ohlig Sekt "50 Degrees N" Brut Weiss, Rheingau

   $$ Weingut Robert Weil Riesling Sekt Brut, Rheingau

   $$ Peter Lauer Reserve Riesling Sekt Vintage Brut, Mosel

3. **Cake Cake Cake Cake: MOSCATO D'ASTI**

Most people think that sweet wine automatically means cheap. That's not always the case, and good Moscato d'Asti is a perfect example of a saccharine sipper misunderstood: It's light, fresh, and a smidge sweet—just the right amount for your fluffy confection. And a cake's sweetness is key here. Why? Foods with higher sugar content tend to make wines taste more bitter than they are. To counteract this, you need a wine that's just as sweet, if not more so, and Moscato's fizz works to make sure the cake's sticky icing is whisked away with each sip. The fluffiness of the cake itself is elevated by the crispness of the wine, its flavors lightened up by the freshness of its fruit bubbles. Bonus points: Moscato d'Asti is low in alcohol (around 4.5 to 5.5 percent), meaning older relatives or family members who don't drink much can imbibe without feeling too uncomfortable.

$ Michele Chiarlo "Nivole" Moscato d'Asti MV

$ La Spinetta "Biancospino," Moscato d'Asti MV

4. **The All-Night Sipper: BRUT NATURE**

The two biggest problems with keeping the bubble train rolling all night are 1) the potential hangover, and 2) the extra calories you take in from a typical bubbly, which has up to 12 grams per liter of residual sugar. However, a sparkling wine with no dosage (no added sugar) solves both problems. Meet Brut Nature, the driest style of sparkler with zero to no more than 3 grams per liter of residual sugar. It's akin to an electric bolt of lightning shooting straight through your palate with scorching citrus and subtle notes in tow; they're delicious, but not for the faint of palate. But let's face it, you and your epic dance moves were born ready for this tongue tango. And on top of saving you calories, your liver will thank you for giving it less sugar to process all night long, softening the effects the morning after.

$ Cava: Juve Y Camps "Reserva de la Familia" Cava Brut Nature

$$ Champagne: Drappier Brut Nature Zero Dosage

$$$ Champagne: Louis Roederer Brut Nature Vintage

5. **The Super-Secret Special Bottle: PRESTIGE CUVÉE CHAMPAGNE**

This is a wine shared solely between the two of you—so this is where you splurge. But before you drop some serious cash, a brief lesson: In the universe of Champagne, there are multi-vintage Champagnes and single-vintage Champagnes. For the latter, the tippy-top quality tier is called a prestige cuvée, or tête de cuvée (tet duh koo-vay). It represents the very best parcels of fruit each Champagne house (a.k.a. winery) uses to make their wares, and is made in infinitesimal quantities compared to other types of Champagne. It also isn't made every year, only when the quality of the singular vintage is high enough.

Most prestige cuvées have a signature name they're known as, not to be confused with the larger Champagne house they come from. For example, Cristal is the signature name, not the name of its house (see below). Prestige cuvées can also be aged longer, and they often have the most complex expression and character style. Which is to say they are dumbfoundingly, bomb-diggity-ly, stupidly good, with layers upon layers of texture, flavor, and aromatics bursting out of the glass and racing through your palate. Which is also to say: Hide it.

$$$ Bollinger "La Grande Année" Brut Vintage

$$$$ Louis Roederer "Cristal" Brut Vintage

$$$$$ Salon Blanc de Blancs "Le Mesnil" Brut Vintage

Run the Kitchen

If there's a part of you that just can't let go of control when having an at-home dinner party, and you're quite confident in your ability to cook for a crowd and stay composed while doing so, then have at it. Here are four menus, one for each season, from Gabrielle Hakman, a chef who's helmed kitchens in Miami and New York. Each menu highlights seasonal fare and serves twelve.

—————— SPRING ——————

Appetizer

RADISH TOAST WITH ANCHOVY-CHIVE BUTTER

MAKES 24 PIECES

1½ cups [3 sticks or 330 g] unsalted butter, at room temperature

6 anchovies, minced

¼ cup [10 g] finely chopped fresh chives or a mix of soft herbs (parsley, dill, tarragon), plus more for garnish

Salt and pepper

24 slices baguette

16 radishes, sliced very thin

Preheat the oven to 325°F [160°C]. In a small bowl, combine the butter, anchovies, and fresh chives and mix until smooth. Season with salt and pepper. Place the baguette slices on a baking sheet and toast in the oven for 7 to 8 minutes. Let cool. Slather the bread with a shmear of butter (roughly 1 tablespoon [14 g] per baguette slice), place some radish slices on top, and garnish with more chives.

Continued

By sticking to what's in season, it's easier to find local, organic produce at the grocery store, or even better, the farmers' market. Out-of-season produce likely had to travel far to reach the shelves, meaning its freshness is questionable and it arrives with a greater carbon footprint.

Main

SLOW-ROASTED SALMON & ASPARAGUS

SERVES 12

Twelve 6 oz [170 g] skin-on salmon fillets

3 lemons

Kosher salt and pepper

3 bunches asparagus

½ cup [65 g] capers

1 cup [40 g] chopped fresh herbs (any mix of parsley, mint, dill, basil, or tarragon)

¾ cup [180 ml] good-quality extra virgin olive oil, plus more for the salmon

Lemon wedges, for garnish

Preheat the oven to 275°F [135°C]. Line two baking sheets with parchment paper.

Drizzle the parchment with olive oil and place the salmon skin-side down on the paper. Zest all of the lemons and set aside whole for the relish. Rub the fillets with more olive oil, the lemon zest, and salt and pepper. Bake for 30 to 40 minutes, until they turn opaque and are slightly firm to the touch. Salmon may be served warm or at room temperature.

While the salmon bakes, fill a pot, large enough to hold all the asparagus, with very salty water. Bring to a boil over high heat. Fill a bowl with cold water and ice. Leaving the asparagus bunches intact, trim about 1 in [2.5 cm] off the bottoms. Place the asparagus in the boiling water and blanch until it turns bright green. This should only take 2 to 3 minutes. Drain, and drop the bunches into the bowl of ice water to cool quickly. After cooling, remove the rubber bands from the asparagus and spread them out on dish towels to dry.

Holding the reserved lemons over a bowl (to catch the juice), remove the segments, discarding as much of the membrane as possible.

Continued

Place the segments in a bowl. Add the capers, chopped herbs, olive oil, and salt and pepper and stir to combine. Add the reserved lemon juice as needed.

To serve, lay the salmon on large platters surrounded by the asparagus and drizzle all with the lemon-caper salsa. Garnish with the lemon wedges.

Signature Cocktail

ELDERFLOWER LAVENDER CHAMPAGNE COCKTAIL

SERVES 12

1 bottle [750 ml] St-Germain liqueur
2 bottles [1.5 L] Champagne
12 oz [360 ml] club soda

Lemon twists, for garnish
Lavender sprigs, for garnish

Pour about 2 oz [60 ml] of St-Germain into a champagne glass. Add at least an equal amount of Champagne or more, depending on taste. Top with 1 oz [30 ml] of club soda and garnish with a curly lemon twist and a sprig of lavender.

Appetizer

TOMATO PEACH CAPRESE SKEWERS

MAKES 24 SKEWERS

48 multicolored baby heirloom tomatoes, about 2 pt [300 g]

6 small peaches, pitted and quartered

24 fresh basil leaves

24 small fresh mozzarella balls, about ½ oz [15 g] each

Flaky sea salt

Extra virgin olive oil

Balsamic glaze

24 decorative bamboo picks

To assemble the skewers, place a tomato, peach slice, basil leaf, mozzarella ball, and contrasting color tomato to finish on each pick. Arrange the skewers on a platter and sprinkle with salt. Drizzle with olive oil and balsamic glaze. If preparing ahead of time, drizzle just before serving.

Main

LOBSTER ROLL SLIDERS

MAKES 24 SANDWICHES

3 lb [1.4 kg] cooked lobster meat, cut into small chunks*

1 cup [240 g] mayonnaise

2 celery stalks, finely minced

2 Tbsp finely minced fresh chives

1 tsp finely minced fresh tarragon

Zest of 1 lemon

1 tsp Old Bay Seasoning

Kosher salt

24 soft slider buns, such as mini-brioche or King's Hawaiian

24 small cornichons

24 cocktail or frilly picks

In a large bowl, gently mix the lobster meat, mayonnaise, celery, herbs, lemon zest, Old Bay, and kosher salt. Taste and adjust the seasoning. Place approximately 2 oz [55 g] of lobster salad on each roll. Place a cornichon on each cocktail pick and use to decoratively secure the sandwich together. Arrange the sliders on a tray. The lobster salad may be made ahead of time and the sandwiches assembled just before serving.

Lobster meat may be bought precooked and frozen from your fishmonger. You could also substitute lump crabmeat or shrimp if your budget doesn't allow for lobster.

Signature Cocktail

STRAWBERRY ROSÉ SPRITZ

SERVES 12

2 pt [680 g] strawberries, sliced, plus more for garnish

2 bottles [1.5 L] rosé wine

1 cup [240 ml] Aperol or Campari*

1 qt [950 ml] club soda

Mint leaves, for garnish

In a large pitcher, muddle and marinate the sliced strawberries in the rosé wine for a few hours. Strain out the strawberries and pour the strained liquid into a punch bowl. Add the Aperol and club soda. Garnish with fresh sliced strawberries and mint leaves.

Aperol will make a sweeter cocktail and Campari a slightly more bitter one.

Appetizer

ROASTED GRAPE CROSTINI

MAKES 24 PIECES

24 slices baguette

2 lb [910 g] red grapes (or mix of green and red), washed and stems removed

¼ cup [60 ml] extra virgin olive oil, plus more for garnish

3 rosemary sprigs, picked, plus whole sprigs for garnish

Kosher salt and pepper

1½ cups [360 g] goat cheese, at room temperature

Flaky sea salt, for garnish

Preheat the oven to 325°F [160°C]. Line two baking sheets with parchment paper.

Place the baguette slices on one of the prepared pans. Bake for 7 minutes or until lightly toasted. Let cool.

Increase the oven temperature to 400°F [200°C]. Place the grapes on the second prepared pan, drizzle with the olive oil, and sprinkle with the rosemary, salt, and pepper. Toss to coat. Roast the grapes for 30 to 40 minutes until almost bursting.

To assemble, shmear the goat cheese on the toasted baguette slices. Top with a spoonful of roasted grapes. Arrange the toasts on a platter and drizzle with olive oil, sprinkle with flaky salt, and garnish with sprigs of rosemary.

Main

BUTTERNUT SQUASH LASAGNA

SERVES 12

4 lb [1.8 kg] butternut squash, peeled, seeded, and cut into ½ in [12 mm] cubes

4 Tbsp [60 ml] olive oil

2 tsp kosher salt

9 Tbsp [125 g] butter

2 Tbsp whole sage leaves (roughly 12 to 14 leaves, depending on size)

½ cup [70 g] flour

5 cups [1.25 L] milk

2 garlic cloves, minced

½ tsp black pepper

Pinch nutmeg

1½ cups [90 g] grated pecorino

12 no-bake lasagna noodles

2 cups [160 g] shredded mozzarella

Preheat the oven to 400°F [200°C]. Line a baking sheet with parchment paper.

Place the cubed butternut squash on the prepared baking sheet, drizzle with the olive oil, sprinkle with 1 tsp of the salt, and toss to coat. Roast until soft but still a bit al dente, approximately 30 minutes. Set aside. Lower the oven temperature to 375°F [190°C].

In a medium saucepan over medium heat, melt the butter. Add whole sage leaves and cook until fragrant and slightly crispy, about 2 to 3 minutes. Remove the leaves and let drain on paper towels to use for garnish later.

Continued

Lower the heat to low. Add the flour to the melted butter and whisk until smooth. Keep whisking for 1 to 2 minutes. Slowly pour in the milk, always whisking to keep the sauce smooth and free of lumps. Add the garlic, pepper, nutmeg, and remaining 1 tsp of salt. Bring the sauce to a simmer and cook, stirring often, until slightly thickened, about 5 to 7 minutes. Turn off the heat, add 1 cup [60 g] of the pecorino cheese, and taste for seasoning. Set aside.

To assemble, spread 1 cup [240 ml] of the béchamel sauce along the bottom of a 9 by 13 in [23 by 33 cm] casserole pan. Lay 3 or 4 lasagna noodles on top to cover the bottom, breaking if needed to fit the pan. Spread one-third of the remaining sauce over the lasagna noodles. Top with half of the cooked butternut squash and 1 cup [80 g] of the mozzarella cheese. Repeat the next layer in exactly the same way. For the last layer, arrange the remaining lasagna noodles as attractively as you can. There can be space between them. Top with the remaining béchamel and the remaining ½ cup [30 g] of grated pecorino. Cover well with foil and bake for 30 minutes.

Remove the foil and continue to bake the lasagna, uncovered, for another 10 minutes or until bubbly and slightly golden on top. Garnish with the crispy sage leaves.

The lasagna may be prepared and assembled, uncooked, ahead of time. Pull out from the refrigerator 1 hour before baking to bring to room temperature.

Signature Cocktail

SPICED CIDER COCKTAIL

SERVES 12

2 qt [2 L] fresh apple cider

1 orange, sliced

3 cinnamon sticks

1 Tbsp whole black peppercorns

4 whole cloves

4 whole star anise pods

1 bay leaf

Lime or lemon juice

Turbinado sugar, for garnish

24 oz [720 ml] bourbon

24 oz [720 ml] ginger beer

12 apple slices, for garnish

The day before serving, bring the apple cider, orange, and all the spices to a simmer in a medium pot. Let simmer for about 10 minutes. Remove from the heat and when cool, place in a pitcher and refrigerate overnight.

To make the cocktail, strain the chilled spiced apple cider. Dip the rim of a highball glass in lime juice and then into turbinado sugar. Fill the glass with ice and pour in 2 oz [60 ml] each of spiced cider and bourbon. Top with 2 oz [60 ml] of ginger beer. Garnish the drink with an apple slice.

APPETIZER

CHARCUTERIE BOARD

Charcuterie boards may be as large and as varied as you like. Cheeses and cured meats taste better at room temperature, so this is a wonderful option for preparing ahead of time—plus, all the ingredients are store bought, so your only task is arranging everything on the platter. Have fun and be creative!

Here are some guidelines on what makes a good board:

Cured Meats and Charcuterie (at least 2 options)
- *Presliced prosciutto, speck, jamon serrano, smoked ham*
- *Presliced salami, soppressata*
- *Whole dried sausages*
- *Pâté, foie gras*

Soft Cheeses (at least 1 or 2 options)
- *Goat cheese, Gorgonzola Dolce*
- *Triple crème (Brie, Camembert, Cambozola)*
- *Robiola, Taleggio, Fontina*

Hard Cheeses (at least 1 or 2 options)
- *Sharp Cheddar, Gouda, Manchego*
- *Pecorino, Parmigiano-Reggiano*

Fruit, Jams, Nuts, Fresh Veggies (at least 2 options)
- *Dried apricots, dates*
- *Fresh grapes, strawberries, sliced apples, figs*
- *Fig jam, quince paste*
- *Marcona almonds, glazed walnuts*
- *Carrots, celery, bell peppers*

Pickles and Olives (at least 2 options)
- *Cornichons*
- *Pickled vegetables*
- *Olives of any kind*
- *Boquerones (white anchovies in vinegar)*
- *Peppadew peppers*

Use the largest board or platter you have, or even use multiple boards if feeding a lot of people. Always serve with assorted crackers or fresh sliced baguettes. Make sure to have the proper utensils: cheese knives, small serving spoons, mini picks, or cocktail forks.

MAIN

RED WINE—BRAISED SHORT RIBS

SERVES 12

This recipe requires a very large Dutch oven or a large, wide braiser. If you don't have either of those, you can also brown your meat and create the base of your sauce in separate pots, and then assemble all ingredients in a large high-sided roasting pan. The cooking vessel should be sturdy so you can safely remove it from the oven. This recipe takes several hours, and could even be made the day before. If so, prepare the gremolata topping fresh before serving.

SHORT RIBS

5 lb [2.3 kg] boneless short ribs, trimmed of excess fat

2 tsp kosher salt

1 tsp black pepper

¼ cup [60 ml] vegetable or canola oil

3 white onions, diced

8 garlic cloves, chopped

¼ cup [55 g] tomato paste

½ cup [70 g] all-purpose flour

1 bottle [750 ml] hearty red wine

1¾ cups [420 ml] beef broth

¼ cup [60 ml] balsamic vinegar

4 sprigs fresh thyme

2 sprigs fresh rosemary

2 bay leaves

2 lb [910 g] baby Yukon gold potatoes

24 baby carrots with tops, peeled

One 12 oz [340 g] bag frozen pearl onions

GREMOLATA

1 cup [60 g] finely minced parsley

2 Tbsp peeled and grated fresh horseradish root

Zest and juice of 1 lemon

2 garlic cloves, grated

Kosher salt and pepper

Continued

To make the short ribs:

Preheat the oven to 325°F [160°C]. Lay the meat out on a baking sheet and bring to room temperature at least 20 minutes before cooking. Season the meat all over with the salt and pepper.

In a large Dutch oven, heat the oil over medium heat until shimmering. Add the meat to the pot without crowding and cook on one side, without moving, until brown, 3 to 4 minutes. When done, flip over and brown the other side. Transfer the meat to a clean baking sheet and repeat until all meat has been seared.

Carefully pour off all but ¼ cup [60 ml] of fat. Add the diced onions to the Dutch oven and sauté over medium-low heat until translucent, about 3 to 5 minutes. Add the minced garlic and cook just until fragrant, about 1 to 2 minutes. Add the tomato paste and stir together well with the onions and garlic. Cook for another minute and then sprinkle with the flour. Keep stirring and cook for another minute.

Deglaze the pot with the red wine, beef stock, and balsamic vinegar. Scrape up any stuck bits from the bottom of the pot and, when the sauce is smooth, add the herb sprigs and bay leaves. Add the meat and its juices to the pot and bring to a gentle boil. Cover tightly with foil and place in the oven; roast for 2 hours.

Remove the pot from the oven, and carefully take off the foil, watching out for escaping steam. Add the potatoes and carrots to the pot, cover again with foil, and put back in the oven to cook for 45 minutes. Remove the Dutch oven and place on top of the stove. Take off the foil and turn the burner to low heat. Add the pearl onions and gently continue to cook until the onions warm up. Taste for seasoning and add salt and pepper as needed. Remove the woody herb sprigs and bay leaves. Skim the fat off the top if greasy.

To make the gremolata:

Combine all the ingredients in a bowl. Do not make far ahead of time or it will get soggy. Sprinkle the stew with the gremolata when serving.

SIGNATURE COCKTAIL

POMEGRANATE SPARKLING PUNCH

SERVES 12

2 bottles [1.5 L] prosecco, Champagne, or sparkling wine

16 oz [480 ml] vodka

16 oz [480 ml] pomegranate juice

8 oz [240 ml] orange juice

Pomegranate seeds

Orange slices

Fresh mint leaves

Combine all the ingredients in a large punch bowl. Serve with ice.

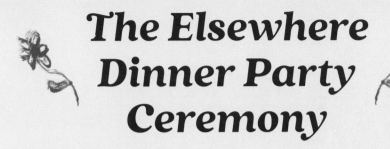

The Elsewhere Dinner Party Ceremony

Don't think you're restricted to your home or a restaurant for your intimate exchanging-of-the-vows followed by food. Depending on your guests' locations and ability to travel, there are many other establishments that will welcome small parties in exchange for a decent rental fee.

Hotels

Many hotels, particularly boutiques, accommodate small weddings—but with very specific parameters regarding the month, and even day of the week, on which they can occur. While you're not likely to reserve a private space in a top hotel on a Saturday between April and October, chances are good you can snag one in off-wedding-season months. Know that not every hotel's kitchen or catering staff will (or is permitted to) work with you on a small menu, though, so before you fall in love with one, call or email the hotel to be sure.

Dive Bars

This one pairs well with courthouse chic. And we're not talkin' those "dive" bars where a PBR pounder is $8, the menu mentions something "artisanal," and the bathrooms are clean. We're talkin' wood-paneled walls laced with decades of cigarette smoke (most are now non-smoking, but it's a good idea to call and check in advance), cracked vinyl barstools, a neon Rolling Rock sign (there's always a neon Rolling Rock sign), and a bartender who greets you with something about the shocks going on her Ford Taurus. Tip her well.

Dive bars make great venues for small parties, but know that by even considering this option, you're agreeing to a menu of fried food that's scribbled on neon poster board and taped up behind the bar. Some even have private rooms you can rent; they often start with "Moose," "Elks," or "Eagles," and end with "Lodge" or "Club."

Something Hip and Alcohol-Forward

Wineries, breweries, and distilleries are all great for off-the-radar wedding celebrations, and some even have fully staffed kitchens with highly skilled chefs running the show. For those that don't, you can usually arrange for a food truck to take care of any vittles for a fraction of what a restaurant would cost.

With any of these spots, make sure they can create a small gathering space for you, whether indoors or out, or else the meaning of the word "intimate" gets sucked right up in their cavernous floor plan.

Northern California has long been renowned for its vineyards and wineries, and now you can find elopement packages at venues within many of the region's coveted twin valleys, Napa and Sonoma. Many have on-site chefs who are experienced catering to intimate-size gatherings.

The Neighborhood Park

Last, this oft-overlooked option is ridiculously simple, sweet, and cheap. Most cities have straight-forward procedures for renting out pavilions in small parks (and also strict policies around alcohol, so be sure to look into this ahead of time). Make it a potluck, fire up the grill, and don't forget the cooler. And ice. Because remember: You always need more ice.

CHAPTER 9:

The Surpris Ceremo

ny

Caroline & Marty

Caroline and Marty were around three months out from holding their engagement party when an idea struck: Why not surprise everyone by using the party to get married on the spot?

"The more we thought about it, the more fun it sounded," says Caroline. "We'd still get to have our fun party, but would eliminate all the pre-wedding stress, and could pick and choose the traditions that felt right for us without the obligations or fuss of a more typical wedding."

They had already locked in the venue for their engagement party, the striking, circa-1890 National Union Building in downtown Washington, DC, which was a perfect fit for gathering around a hundred loved ones for the surprise. Their plan was to have guests arrive and gather on the first floor, where a full bar and appetizers would be served. Caroline and Marty would greet everyone, mingle, and sip their signature cocktails, a French 75 for her and a whiskey sour for him, then disappear to connect with their photographer and officiant.

One crucial decision they'd made beforehand was to tell their parents. Marty told his family the night before the party. ("They were excited," he says, "but didn't have much of a choice, since they'd already come into town for the party.")

Caroline's parents were also excited; her mom had a lot of questions about how the surprise would work, and her dad thought it was a great idea too, but wanted to make sure he could still walk her down the aisle (both parents did) and give a toast. Caroline's sister thought the idea was fun, but still wanted her to have a full, traditional wedding.

Caroline wasn't too worried about the surprise element from the get-go—her parents had also had a nontraditional wedding and were married at home on New Year's Eve with just their closest friends. Whether her parents knew it or not, Caroline felt that their 1988 decision gave her permission to continue the family tradition of breaking tradition.

After about an hour and a half of mingling, Marty and Caroline took to the grand staircase with microphones in hand to make a "toast." Marty said to the room, "Thank you all for coming to our engagement party, but what you're really here for is to witness our wedding!" There was shrieking, jumping, and clapping. Caroline's Aunt Nancy burst into tears and didn't stop crying for the entire ceremony.

"The feeling of watching our friends and family react to the news is one neither of us will ever forget," says Caroline. "It was pure happiness."

Caroline & Marty's Fine Print

LIVE: Alexandria, Virginia

WORK: Caroline is a Medicare health plan manager, and Marty works in health care sales.

AGES WHEN THEY ELOPED: She was twenty-eight, and he was forty-three.

MARTY'S FIRST IMPRESSION: "I remember thinking she was very pretty but too young for me—and too smart."

CAROLINE'S FIRST IMPRESSION: "I wasn't disappointed."

RELATIONSHIP TIME LINE: Dated for around two years → Engaged for six months → Eloped June 2018 → Honeymooned November through December 2018

PROPOSAL: Marty popped the question on New Year's Eve at a Spoon concert at the 9:30 Club in DC (a famous music venue they frequented). Says Caroline: "It was perfect."

WEDDING VENUE: National Union Building, Washington, DC.

DISTANCE FROM HOME TO VENUE: 8 miles / 12.9 km

NUMBER OF GUESTS: 100

SHE WORE: A sparkly, champagne-colored cocktail dress from BHLDN

HE WORE: A blue suit that he already owned and a matching bow tie he snagged for $20 at Nordstrom

VOWS: It was important to Marty and Caroline that their vows be unique and reflective of their values. They used a back-and-forth format where they alternated reading lines about their commitment to equal partnership and supporting each other's dreams

SPENT: $32,055

BIGGEST SPLURGE: $10,000 on the venue.

WHAT THEY DID WITH THE MONEY THEY SAVED: Booked first-class tickets to Southeast Asia

A RUNDOWN OF CAROLINE AND MARTY'S VENDORS

Officiant: A close friend who's "an excellent secret-keeper"

Photographer: Chosen specifically for her photojournalistic style

Florist: Whom they worked closely with for their "romantic yet organic-looking" centerpieces

Food: Kept to just appetizers catered by a local company

Cake: Three tiers of chocolate, vanilla, and coconut

Entertainment: Spotify, played from an iPhone through the venue's sound system

Day-of coordinator: Whose husband graciously managed the sound system

If you're pivoting to a surprise wedding, tell your photographer over the phone, says Bonnie Sen, Caroline and Marty's photographer. That way, nothing's lost in translation, as it could be over email.

Why You Should Have a Surprise Ceremony

Everyone loves a good surprise, and the next best thing after getting a surprise is giving a surprise. The anticipation of the "gotcha" moment is exciting for you both, and your guests will love it. With zero expectations and no wedding constructs, everyone can truly relax.

How to Pull It Off

- Get engaged. Sit back and bask in the congrats.

- Pick a date. Aim for one that's two to three months after the proposal, while loved ones are still amped for you.

- Decide on the venue. This will largely depend on your date and how many guests you want to invite, but once you have an idea of both, lock in the venue.

- Alert any vendors you already hired. If you intend on asking a vendor to make the pivot from working your big wedding to a brand-new date with a scaled-down format (and budget), be flexible and overly gracious—you're now messing with their schedule, and the ball is *entirely* in their court. Be willing to part with vendors, if necessary. Still leave them a good review.

- If you can, hang on to your wedding coordinator, as wiggling plans is in her wheelhouse, and she can quickly tap her network to replace any key vendors who have to bail.

- Decide on guests. If you haven't yet sent out save-the-dates for your would-be wedding, go ahead and invite whomever you'd like. If you've already sent save-the-dates, it's highly recommended that you invite everyone who received one.

- Create a cover story and stick with it. You'll need a roster of fake wedding updates to share when people ask. Don't let your partner veer off-script.

How to Drop the Matrimonial Bomb

It's not as simple as opening a door and yelling "Surprise!" but by "borrowing" one of these other occasions, your secret plan will go off without a hitch (so you can, you know, get hitched).

The "Proposal"

This one is a surprise double whammy: Your guests have been invited by the bride or groom to witness a surprise proposal to you, the unsuspecting-but-in-the-know partner. In reality, the proposal has already been done, and what they're really showing up for is your wedding. Unlike other types of surprise weddings, this format allows (one of) you to give guests a heads-up on the details and lead them to believe that they're in on the ruse (uncles love a good ruse), when, in fact, they're actually in for a wild surprise.

Engagement Party

If you're already headed down the path of wedding planning, follow Caroline and Marty's lead and, if the timing's right, flip your engagement party into a surprise ceremony. Doing so will create a more intimate gathering of family and friends; it's hands down the easiest way to get everyone together without suspicion; and it's the best option if many of your guests live out of town. The cocktail hour format works well here as guests are distracted by the open bar and won't notice when you disappear to prep for the Big Moment.

Hijack a Holiday

OK, probably don't do this on a major holiday, but by planning a surprise ceremony on a more innocuous occasion such as Mother's Day, you're able to get your parents and siblings to come together without suspecting anything. Gift them hotel rooms in your city and, on the side, plan a ceremony on the hotel's property. However, do not hijack the actual holiday you've gathered them for. Instead, aim to get everyone in town early and host a brunch or dinner that functions as the surprise ceremony the day before or after the actual holiday.

Or, for the brave few out there, hit them with the news around a more significant—but low-pressure—holiday, such as Thanksgiving Eve, the unofficial drinking night of the holiday season, or a Fourth of July barbecue, when the mood is jovial and you won't spoil anyone's day with your big news. Out of respect, avoid religious holidays.

Housewarming Party

This ruse works well for two obvious reasons: You have something to celebrate, and you are in total control of the environment.

Housewarming parties are casual and fun, and usually come with no expectations from the guests—they're mainly there for the free snacks and alcohol, making the surprise nuptials all the more exciting. Here, the more the merrier, so it's less obvious when you both dip into your bedroom to do Fireball shots before making The Announcement.

CHAPTER 10:

The Second

Wedding

Shelby & Kyle

For Shelby's second marriage, she knew exactly what kind of ceremony she didn't want—anything that even slightly resembled her first one: "Your traditional, invite one hundred fifty people, get married on the beach, have a reception in a little art gallery, have a DJ and bridesmaids, and wear a traditional white wedding dress. From David's Bridal."

She was still married when she started a new job in September 2016, which is where she met her now-husband, Kyle. They both worked in the IT department, and she remembers thinking he was cute, but nothing more. He considered her purely "coworker zoned" because she was married.

Around a month after Shelby started the job, she separated from her husband. At work, she became a bit more social, she says, going to lunches, then happy hours, then trivia nights, all the while getting to know Kyle and developing a "monster crush" on him. ("I'm pretty sure he had a crush on me too.")

It got to the point where she felt like they were becoming cochairs of an events committee that didn't exist, constantly planning work outings just so they could hang out together. Eventually, she says, it got to a "fever pitch," and they finally went on a real first date outside of work, a casual lunch on a late Saturday afternoon.

In February 2018, after seven months of dating, they got engaged. While walking their dog one day, Shelby mentioned that for her thirty-third birthday, she'd like to have a baby. Kyle said for that to happen, they'd have to get married.

The following month, Shelby turned the annual family vacation to St. Simons Island with her aunt, uncle, sister, and sister's husband into an opportunity for an elopement. The timing was incredibly fortuitous, as Shelby's sister was pregnant and due the following June, and wouldn't be able to travel in the foreseeable future. She and Shelby are extremely close; their father passed away in 2011, and their mother had been estranged for most of their adult lives (she passed away while they were on this vacation, which they learned when they got home).

The day of the ceremony, a warm Thursday in mid-March, everyone walked from the condo to a park down the street, where Shelby and Kyle were married by her uncle under a thick oak tree covered with moss. Kyle's parents were also there, and afterward, once the hugging and crying were over, they walked to dinner to celebrate.

What did Kyle think of the low-key affair? At first, he says, "I didn't really think we 'eloped,' because I considered eloping to be people who have just met within the past day or two getting married while intentionally not telling people they know. Shelby, and the dictionary, have since helped me see how others define it.

"I wouldn't do anything differently, even with this new definition."

THE SECOND WEDDING

Shelby & Kyle's Fine Print

LIVE: St. Petersburg, Florida

WORK: Shelby is an operations manager, and Kyle is an enterprise application analyst manager.

AGES WHEN THEY ELOPED: Both were thirty-three.

RELATIONSHIP TIME LINE: Dated for seven months → Engaged for a month → Eloped March 2018

PROPOSAL: Says Kyle: "We did have a 'makeup' proposal dinner. While Shelby was getting ready for it, I lit a bunch of candles in the next room and asked in a more traditional sense. It's not that stressful once you've already heard the answer."

WEDDING VENUE: Mallery Park on St. Simons Island

DISTANCE FROM HOME TO VENUE: 298 miles / 480 km

NUMBER OF GUESTS: 7

SHE WORE: A Halston Heritage, Blush Imprint Dress from Rent the Runway

HE WORE: A navy blue button-down shirt, pink tie, sneakers he already owned, and newish khakis. "Kyle's a very thrifty person," says Shelby. "I had to *negotiate* with him to buy a new pair of khakis." He caved, but only because she bought them at the thrift store.

RING: They bought an opal ring Shelby had been eyeing for the engagement, along with a small gold wedding band. Kyle has a rubber ring.

VOWS: Around a week before their elopement, Shelby and Kyle wrote their vows together in a card she purchased from a local card maker. They included a line from a song called "Vintage" by High Dive Heart: "I love you more today than I did yesterday / I will love you more tomorrow than I do today."

SPENT: $800

WHAT THEY DID WITH THE MONEY THEY SAVED: Put it toward the down payment on their house.

Why Have a Second Wedding?

First of all, who cares what the haters think: If you want another one-hundred-fifty-person wedding with all of its trappings, do it. But if you're reading this, chances are you want to do something more *you*, more laid-back, and free of any Instagram hashtags that will never go away.

If your first wedding was about managing the expectations of others, this one gets to be all yours. Cheers to new beginnings.

> For your engagement ring, consider incorporating pearls, which are believed to nurture new beginnings.

Traditions to Make Your Own

Just because you've already done the garter toss once doesn't mean you have to toss every tradition out the window. Here's what to keep and what to make your own, now that you're older and wiser.

The Bridal Shower

This is a highly charged and divisive topic. Some friends and family members won't understand why you want to have another bridal shower and might resent buying you a gift this go-round. But there's no need to be hard on yourself for wanting a second shower, or even needing one if you lost some essentials in your divorce—just don't wait around for someone else to host it, unless they offer. The etiquette put forth by the Emily Post Institute advises that you keep the guest count small, and the registry too.

Bachelor and Bachelorette Parties

Rather than having traditional, gender-specific parties, consider planning an event that brings members of both bridal parties and families together to meet before the rehearsal dinner (if you're having one). Throw a party at home or get everyone together for a weekend doing something you love, which might be as all-out as a ski trip or as laid-back as an evening of bowling.

The White Dress

The whole white dress thing is believed to symbolize purity and virginity. Wear it if you'd like, or feel empowered to wear any other color out there. Splurge on that floor-length gown with Art Deco beading or that boho watercolor maxi dress. Wear black.

Something Old/New/ Borrowed/Blue

First, skip the "something old," which represents the bride's past. Instead, focus on "something new," which represents the future; "something borrowed," which is supposed to bring good luck; and "something blue," which symbolizes fidelity and love. And, while

INCLUDING THE KIDS

If either (or both) of you have kids, it's important to let them know they're part of your new union. There are many ways to include them in your second wedding that will create sweet, lasting memories for you *and* them.

- A great format to consider is a destination elopement, which will feel like a vacation for the kids (and for you too).
- If they're little, give them a role so they feel included: let them play ring bearer or flower girl, be the best man or maid of honor, or walk you down the aisle.
- Incorporate a symbolic ritual to show unity, such as lighting a mother-son candle together during the ceremony.
- Reserve the first dance for your daughter or son.
- Or, if dancing is your jam, do a choreographed dance together to something fun and upbeat.
- Let them make a toast or give a speech. Whatever their age, it's sure to be memorable.
- If they're older, bring them in on the planning and let them make some decisions, such as what songs to put on the playlist or what the dessert should be.

traditionally worn by the bride, why not both take part?

Smash Cake in Each Other's Faces—or Don't

This messy tradition dates back to ancient Rome, when brides had barley cake crumbled on their heads to symbolize good fortune and fertility. Feel free to say no thank you to this—you don't need to ruin a second wedding dress, or a $12 slice of wedding cake.

Bouquet Toss

Have fun here and only invite divorcées to participate to see who you'll be passing the second wedding baton to.

How to Legally Get Married a Second (or "Another") Time

While your second wedding might feel far more carefree than your first, there are some very important legal steps to take as you prepare to tie the knot again.

The Paperwork

When you head to the courthouse to get a marriage license for the second time, don't forget to take your divorce decree or certificate of dissolution from your previous marriage (usually just referred to as "divorce papers"). It should've arrived by mail after your divorce was finalized, but if you misplaced it, have your lawyer request a copy, as you absolutely cannot get a marriage license without proof of the divorce.

When you head to the courthouse, have on hand the following information:

- The exact date of your divorce.
- The state or country where the divorce was ordered (often seen in this context as "decreed").
- The specific grounds for divorce.

Your ex doesn't need to be present or provide anything to the court in order for you to apply for a new marriage license. (If your former spouse is deceased, you need to provide evidence of that, which is usually in the form of a death certificate.)

If you're divorced and your old wedding band is tucked away behind your loose socks, now is as good a time as any to get rid of it (before acquiring another one). Aside from returning it (which you should do if it is a family heirloom), the noblest thing you can do is donate it to a nonprofit that can "repurpose" it to support their causes. There are many hospitals, women's advocacy nonprofits, and veteran organizations that do this.

Divorce Waiting Period

Just as there's a waiting period to get married in some states, there's also a waiting period when you divorce. It starts the moment you legally file your papers, and like its predecessor, the purpose of a divorce waiting period is to provide couples a window of time to ponder the question, *Are you sure you want to do this?*

QUICKIE DIVORCES

The same legislation that Nevada governor Fred B. Balzar signed in 1931 to legalize gambling and entice lovers to elope to Vegas also created the most lenient divorce laws in the country. During the 1930s, thousands of scorned spouses—particularly celebrities day-tripping from California—poured into the City of Second Chances to take advantage of the six-week waiting period, which at the time was the shortest in the country (today there is none).

CHAPTER 11

Eloping During

Hard
Times

Bri & Lindsey

What was supposed to happen was this: Bri and Lindsey would get married beneath a magnificent oak tree outside of Hotel Ella, a Greek revival mansion-turned-boutique-hotel in downtown Austin, surrounded by one hundred loved ones. It would happen on April 10, 2020 (which was also Good Friday, "because nothing says 'He is Risen' like a good ol' lesbian wedding," jokes Lindsey). They had "a menu that would make your toes curl," elegant linen and china, perfect floral centerpieces, dried bridal bouquets with hints of Bri's favorite wildflowers, and thoughtfully curated playlists for the ceremony, cocktail hour, and dance-party reception. "We had intention behind every single detail of our wedding," says Lindsey.

Instead, they said their vows on April 28, 2020, atop a shaky make-shift stage in the gravel parking lot of a drive-in movie theater in a dot of a town outside Austin. Something like ninety cars showed up, but Bri and Lindsey had no idea who was actually *inside* the cars, since it was difficult to peer in, what

with social distancing in place. The menu included mini corn dogs, popcorn, and soda. They traded their heels for cowboy boots, which caused their dresses to drag in the dirt since there was no time to get them hemmed. "We never thought we'd be getting married on a Tuesday during a global pandemic at a drive-in movie theater in Buda, Texas," says Lindsey. "But everything about it fit us."

The two met on a lesbian dating app in June 2018. Within twelve hours of matching with Lindsey, Bri asked her on a date to an outdoor concert at Zilker Park in Austin, where they both live. "It only took me three days to ask her to be my girlfriend, five days to tell her I loved her (in true lesbian fashion), one year to move in together, thirteen months to propose to her, and less than two years to marry her," says Bri.

A little more than a year after their first date, in July 2019, they officially kicked off wedding planning by putting down the deposit for Hotel Ella, a favorite venue of Lindsey's, as she'd sang there at many weddings during her professional Christian singing career. She and Bri spent the rest of 2019 hiring a photographer, videographer, florist, cake vendor, even a cotton candy spinning duo called The Cotton Candy Cowgirls. Countless painstaking hours went into planning their dream wedding.

Then, as 2019 rolled into 2020, news of a novel coronavirus started trickling into mainstream media outlets. In early March, Americans everywhere were glued to their screens, stripping grocery store aisles of toilet paper and Clorox wipes in mass preparation for the unknown. On March 11, 2020, the World Health Organization declared the coronavirus a global pandemic, and as cases in the US surpassed one thousand, public officials began canceling events big and small—including most weddings.

On March 25, while Bri cooked dinner for their three kids (Bri's son and Lindsey's adopted twin girls), Lindsey sat and dug into the latest coronavirus news, which is when she saw the shelter-in-place order for Austin. It had gone into effect the night before and was to last until at least April 13—three days after their wedding date. In that moment, she says, "My stomach

sank along with my heart. It was a different sad. The kind that knocks the breath out of you." Until that point, she and Bri had held onto the hope that nothing would get in the way of their dream wedding day. But as Lindsey digested the details of the order and did more research, reality slowly began to sink in. Their wedding, just two weeks away, clearly would not be happening.

In the following days, they felt "frozen without any ability to pivot gracefully," says Lindsey. "Schedules weren't aligning, vendors weren't coordinating, and waiting until 2021 was not an option either of us wanted to explore."

The day of their original wedding, they decided to go on a date. With everything closed—restaurants, parks, trails—they drove to the top of an empty parking garage, ordered pizza, and polished off a bottle of Champagne. As the sun set, they shared impromptu vows, promises they wanted to make to each other as they awaited their new wedding date, whenever that might be.

The next morning, while watching cartoons with their kids, Bri saw a commercial for Doc's Drive In Theatre in nearby Buda. "Our hearts lit up," says Lindsey. After a phone call with the owners of the drive-in, followed by an excited call to their wedding planner, "It was all hands on deck."

First, they had to figure out a date. This revolved largely around the schedule of one of Lindsey's closest friends, author Jen Hatmaker, whom they wished to be their officiant but who was in the midst of releasing her latest book while moving her book tour online. It was "the logistical Olympics," says Lindsey, but they made it work, and settled on Tuesday, April 28.

Then Bri and Lindsey began re-inviting everyone to their new wedding. Since the drive-in could hold 90 cars, they were able to open up their guest list significantly, inviting more friends than they ever could have afforded to have at their original wedding.

They were able to re-secure their original photographer and videographer, while hunting down a second videographer who was also an expert in nighttime lighting; the ceremony didn't start until 8:30 p.m., and they needed the entire experience to be projected onto two movie screens. For sound, they were able to bring on a singer/songwriter friend to help with A/V.

After getting ready in a "tiny home" behind the movie screens, Lindsey walked down the gravel aisle with her twin girls, flanked by forty-five cars on each side, an instrumental version of "Hallelujah" by Leonard Cohen playing the entire time. Then Bri walked down the aisle, watching Lindsey, on-screen, as she stood waiting for her on the stage. "Miraculously, we were able to show the ceremony on the movie screens and send the audio feed into everyone's cars," says Lindsey. "I still can't believe we pulled it off, especially with the livestreaming element"—they were able to broadcast their wedding on Instagram, Facebook Live, and YouTube to thousands of friends and family who couldn't be there.

During their vows, Lindsey surprised Bri with a song she'd written for her; Bri wrote special vows for Lindsey's daughters, "a major tearjerker, as you can imagine," says Lindsey. As they shared their first kiss as wives, the inky sky surrounding them, cars honked, and they looked out at the dusty parking lot as if they had forgotten where they were—at a drive-in, on a big screen, in front of hundreds of friends and strangers, all sharing this singular moment of joy in what was one of the most uncertain periods of their collective lives.

They ended the ceremony on a lighthearted note with the song "Club Going Up On A Tuesday" by the artist iLoveMakonnen (later, he heard that they'd used his song during their ceremony and sent them an "encouraging email"). At the end of the night, in true pandemic fashion, "We essentially had to kick the guests out of the theater because of the local curfew that was in place," says Lindsey.

Looking back, what advice do they have for couples who have to cancel their dream weddings due to unforeseen events? "Hold your plans loosely. Let go when the opportunity presents itself. If you let love lead, and you live with your whole heart trusting in the process and trusting the path no matter how 'off' it may seem, you will end up where you're supposed to be.

"Love is enough."

Bri & Lindsey's Fine Print

LIVE: Austin, Texas

WORK: Bri is a certified health coach and CEO/founder of HERgoods, and Lindsey is a director of wealth management at a boutique financial planning firm. ("We are both also unpaid taxi drivers for three tiny humans.")

AGES WHEN THEY ELOPED: Bri was thirty-one, and Lindsey was thirty-seven.

LINDSEY'S FIRST IMPRESSION: "Apps are hard. But then the night before my birthday, I saw the most enchanting woman I'd *ever* laid my eyes on. She was photographed in front of a green wall that happened to be my favorite shade of green, sitting cross-legged like the modern badass woman she is. I instantly thought, *I don't know what a catfish really is, but I feel like this is that.* However, I couldn't keep myself from scrolling through more of her photos. She had the kindest, most beautiful brown eyes,

and I could see her loving heart through all her photos. Plus she was wearing the sexiest Open Road Stetson hat I'd ever seen."

BRI'S FIRST IMPRESSION: "A blond-haired, green-eyed single mom of twins with the most beautiful smile I'd ever seen— and someone who desperately *hates* mayonnaise (according to her profile), had no intentions of getting married, having more kids, or casually hooking up. I found myself captivated yet skeptical."

RELATIONSHIP TIME LINE: Dated for thirteen months → Engaged for eight months (from when Bri proposed) and six months (from when Lindsey proposed) → Original wedding date: April 10, 2020 → Eloped: April 28, 2020

PROPOSAL: Bri proposed in August 2019 during the Austin Pride Festival at a rooftop bar where she'd secretly invited Lindsey's friends, family, and coworkers. Lindsey proposed the following October during the Albuquerque International Balloon Fiesta, which was canceled due to extreme fog. Instead of proposing in the basket of a hot-air balloon during sunrise, Lindsey got down on one knee on the ground while Bri was being interviewed by a camera crew. Lindsey managed to show the camerawoman a message on her phone saying she was going to propose, and the whole thing was captured and shown on the evening news.

WEDDING VENUE: Doc's Drive In Theatre

DISTANCE FROM HOME TO VENUE: 15 miles / 24 km

NUMBER OF GUESTS: Ninety cars came to the drive-in, maxing out its capacity, and Bri and Lindsey estimate that there were three to four people in each car. Thousands attended virtually.

BRI WORE: A dress from BHLDN in Chicago and a hat from Maufrais in downtown Austin

LINDSEY WORE: A dress from Second Summer Bridal in Austin and also a hat from Maufrais

RINGS: Bri took a two-carat diamond ring that was gifted to Lindsey in 2009 from a stranger on a plane (true story) and modernized it, adding fifty small diamonds around the original stone placed on a simple gold band. Lindsey had Bri's ring custom made, a pear-shaped diamond measuring a tad over two carats.

SPENT: The drive-in wedding cost between $10,000 and $15,000. (Lindsey says she doesn't want to look at the exact figures since she's a penny-pincher.) They didn't lose any money on their original wedding.

HONEYMOON: They swapped their ten-day honeymoon in Tulum for a two-day mini-moon at Casita Coyote, a cliffside hideaway outside of Austin where they stayed in an Airstream trailer, listened to records, grilled, drank, and laughed.

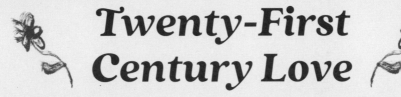

Twenty-First Century Love

This century has ushered in a wave of circumstances that have made the simple and beautiful act of getting married quite difficult—if not impossible. In 2001, the United States entered into a decades-long war following the attacks on the Twin Towers, sending hundreds of thousands of troops overseas while separating couples for unknown periods of time. This created a wave of wartime weddings not seen since World War II.

In 2008, the Great Recession hit, pushing couples into financial hardship that led to majorly scaled-back weddings in a time when budgets had been pushing the $30,000 mark. In the 2010s, changes to immigration policy created lengthy wait times for acquiring a green card, leaving couples in limbo and often separated across continents.

And then came 2020, which saw the worst pandemic in a hundred years completely transform our lives and put a hard stop to travel and large gatherings, and, therefore, weddings.

DEPRESSION BRIDES VS. RECESSION BRIDES

During the last hundred years, the United States has experienced two significant periods of extreme economic collapse: the Great Depression in the late 1920s and 1930s, and the Great Recession nearly a century later. Each impacted how couples got married—particularly how much they spent. Here's a side-by-side look at weddings during each era.

THE GREAT DEPRESSION

HEADLINE: "June Wedding Rush Retarded by Slump," *New York Times*, June 2, 1932

AVERAGE WEDDING COST: $392.30 ($7,341.71 in today's dollars, when adjusted for inflation)

MOST POPULAR MONTH TO GET MARRIED: June

WEDDING DRESS: White rayon gowns that could be dyed and worn again.

HERO FOR THE TIMES: In 1933, President Franklin Roosevelt signed the Cullen-Harrison Act, ending Prohibition and giving couples everywhere something to toast to—and with.

CELEB ELOPEMENT: In March 1939, during a break from filming *Gone With the Wind*, Hollywood legends Clark Gable and Carole Lombard took a drive to Kingman, Arizona, where they eloped.

THE GREAT RECESSION

HEADLINE: "Love in the Time of Recession," *New York Times*, February 9, 2010

AVERAGE WEDDING COST: $29,644

MOST POPULAR MONTH TO GET MARRIED: June

WEDDING DRESS: Simple, A-line dresses replaced the over-the-top ball gowns of the early aughts.

HERO FOR THE TIMES: To help couples who canceled their weddings due to financial hardship, New York photographer Goran

Veljic created elopement company NY1 Minute Weddings, providing professional portraits at steep discounts for couples marrying at the marriage bureau.

CELEB ELOPEMENT: Supermodel Gisele Bündchen and quarterback Tom Brady secretly married at St. Monica Catholic Church with only immediate family in attendance. Afterward, they threw an intimate backyard barbecue at home to celebrate, with Brady helming the grill.

Love in the Time of Coronavirus

Throughout 2020, weddings around the world were affected by the rapidly spreading novel coronavirus. In March of that year, the Centers for Disease Control and Prevention advised that gatherings of fifty people or more be banned for eight weeks, stretching into May, i.e., the unofficial start of wedding season. Then, in many states, indoor gatherings were restricted to no more than ten. Weddings around the world were swiftly canceled or postponed. "Change the Date" cards fluttered through the mail.

This was all incredibly devastating for so many couples like Bri and Lindsey who had been planning their weddings for months, putting down hefty deposits on venues and tasting cake and selecting fonts for save-the-dates and effectively putting together the pieces of a shared future that would launch from this one beautiful day.

Some couples, however, chose to stick with their planned wedding dates, and got married in courthouses, parks, and backyards, keeping in mind the CDC's social-distancing protocol of maintaining a 6 ft [1.8 m] distance from others and wearing the requisite face masks. They worked with their original vendors on revising how their weddings would now look—and cost. Zoom evolved from a way to hold virtual meetings to a platform for sharing these endearing, makeshift nuptials with loved ones around the world (meeting ID still required).

If nothing else, couples made it work. Things looked incredibly different, but wedding season ushered on. And as it did, we saw couples distill their weddings down to the very basics of commitment, and doing so with the kind of ingenuity that tends to surface during difficult times. Here are some of our favorite ideas that sprung out of the pandemic, which deserve a permanent place on wedding planning inspiration boards for years to come.

The Stoop Wedding

You don't need to live in Brooklyn to have a fab stoop wedding. The key here is to go big—as in huge—with florals. This looks best as a floral installation framing your doorway and, subsequently, you, as you stand on your steps for stoop nuptials, loved ones watching from below. Then, by all means, have a dance party in the street. (If you're looking for inspiration, just Google "Elaine Welteroth wedding"—the former *Teen Vogue* editor held a gorgeous stoop wedding in May 2020 that's essentially the blueprint for all others.

The Front Porch Wedding

The stoop wedding's cousin, the front porch wedding offers more in the way of space, for one, as well as a roof should it rain. Here, blitz it with twinkle lights and pose for the sweetest photos on the porch swing. Don't have a porch? Wrap-around porches on historic estates make for great mini venues.

The Five-Star Wedding

Hotels and resorts that were previously out-of-reach, pricewise, for a two-hundred-fifty-person wedding are now accessible thanks to the addition of intimate wedding and elopement options due to the pandemic. Bonus: Many five-star venues have kitchens that are helmed by notable chefs, and with a guest list of ten, you can now afford to splurge on a $100-a-plate menu.

The Great Outdoors-ish Wedding

Many mountain lodges, ski resorts, and other Great Outdoors–adjacent venues debuted incredible all-inclusive weekend elopement packages due to the pandemic. Think mimosas in hot tubs and fireside naps—all for the price of a one-day ski pass.

The New Guest List

One thing that nearly all couples who chose to get married during the pandemic faced was cutting

their guest list—and the dreaded announcement that came with it. While the pandemic was an extremely valid excuse to trim the guest count, there are other, more common reasons couples may decide to drop from two hundred and fifty guests to twenty five—stress, money, or just a change of heart, to name a few.

If you find yourself in a situation where you're suddenly narrowing your guest list, here are a few tips: Always prioritize immediate family members and anyone you had asked to be in your wedding party (and their significant others). If you'd like, keep your wedding party the same when you go small. Then think about those in your life who will be there for you in the long haul (incidentally, these are the people who are most likely to understand your decision to go small). This might mean inviting your best friend from college over your first aunt.

A Note on Zoom Weddings

In the early weeks of the pandemic, scores of couples who were determined to keep their wedding dates turned their long-planned, large-scale weddings into quickie elopements that looked a lot like the two of them in a living room, livestreaming with their officiant as their family members and friends watched from the safety of their own homes.

However, one major oversight was that in most states, officiants *must be present in person* to make the marriage legal, meaning many of those Zoom, Skype, or FaceTime nuptials were not actually legal. And the mass majority of couples and officiants didn't seem to know this.

Organizations such as American Marriage Ministries (AMM), which offers online ordination, were inundated with calls and emails from officiants and couples seeking guidance here. AMM ultimately issued a press release to major wedding and bridal outlets to clarify what they knew from their own legal counsel: that the issue with virtual weddings stems from the inability to verify the couple's identity and whether the marriage license is legitimate (*seems important*). The press release states: "In order to ensure that this is done properly, states require that the officiant be physically present to sign and complete the marriage license—which has to occur promptly after the ceremony.

"While virtual ceremonies allow guests to witness the wedding from afar, states typically require that the officiant is physically present with the couple to sign and complete the marriage license, along with witnesses (if needed), immediately following the ceremony."

Three months into the pandemic, those fun kids over at Domino's rolled out an apropos "Rain Check Registry" to accompany their original wedding registry (see page 37). Friends and relatives can buy couples eGift cards such as: "Small Wedding Now, Big Celebration Later," "The OG Wedding Day!," and our personal favorite, "The 'You Taught A Relative How to Video Call' Grand Prize."

As it became clear that the pandemic was here to stay for the foreseeable future, some counties and states began legalizing virtual weddings if conducted remotely by officials such as judges. Overall, remember that marriage laws vary across the country, and during uncertain times, always seek the counsel of a legal expert who specializes in family law before proceeding with a (hopefully legal) virtual ceremony.

Remembering That One Crucial Detail: The Marriage License

In the bustle to replan, reschedule, and rehire, it's imperative not to overlook the one thing that actually makes any of this legal: the marriage license. When wedding plans unexpectedly change, it's important to keep a few things top of mind.

Expiration Date

First things first: Did your marriage license expire? Aren't sure? If you've postponed and are in a replanning phase, check this pronto. Whatever you do, do *not* lock things in with any vendors you may have fallen in love with until you know if your marriage license will still be valid on your new date. If it won't be, get things legally squared away first.

Location

Did you switch the state in which you're having your legal union? Then you must apply for your marriage license in the new state where you plan on getting legally hitched. Remember, marriage licenses don't transfer from state to state (see page 138).

Waiting Period

If you've rescheduled your date and moved your venue to a new state, be sure to look into the waiting period there. US laws regarding the waiting period vary by state. (This is important if you decide to road trip it from Wisconsin to New Orleans for a quickie elopement, for example, since Louisiana has a twenty-four-hour waiting period.)

During the pandemic, many officiants began bringing brand-new pens to every ceremony in order to prevent the spread of germs as the marriage license was passed around for signing. This is a sweet idea we suggest keeping—consider buying a special pen for signing your own marriage license, which then becomes an additional memento from your special day. We suggest a calligraphy or fountain pen, which look *quite* classy in photos.

COMFORT IN TRADITION

According to Eleni N. Gage, author of *Lucky in Love: Traditions, Customs & Rituals to Personalize Your Wedding*, rituals and traditions can have a bonding effect on a couple, leading to greater commitment and more satisfaction in their relationship. They also bring a degree of comfort in uncertain times—and, we like to believe, luck. Here are five auspicious rituals to consider incorporating into your elopement, especially if it's in the midst of a difficult time:

- Handfasting, common in many cultures—most notably Scottish—involves joining hands and having the officiant tie them together with a ribbon, signifying unity. The practice often takes place outdoors and is where we get the phrases "tie the knot" and "hand in marriage."
- Drinking from the same glass of wine during the ceremony represents a shared future. Wine also represents fertility, joy, and revelry.
- If you're having a coastal elopement, a sand ceremony is a sweet way to signify commitment. Each partner pours a vial or cup of sand into a shared glass, and, once mingled, the sand becomes impossible to divide. (Remember to be sensitive to the environment and your surroundings, and don't take too much sand.)
- Jumping the broom is believed to have started with the Roma in Wales around 1700; their weddings weren't recognized by the church, so couples jumped over a broom to signify entering a union together. In the 1800s, these "broomstick weddings" were adopted by enslaved people who could not legally wed. Today, many couples, particularly in Black communities, embrace the tradition: The couple holds hands and hops over a broom after they say their vows.
- The evil eye exists in many cultures as a representation of bad luck. Mirrors are believed to deflect the evil eye back at its giver, so consider hanging small framed mirrors from tree branches or placing them on tables. Or wear them—sequins count too.

Love Is Enough

On March 28, 2020, Sagal and Geoffrey stopped into a Trader Joe's on what was supposed to be their black-tie-optional, rooftop wedding at the Miami Beach Botanical Garden, a day "surrounded by nature, art, dope beats, and the most important people in our lives," they had written on their Zola website. "We are thrilled to have you all join us from every corner of the globe, putting your lives and plans on hold to celebrate this union of love."

But by March 28, beaches, bars, and restaurants had shuttered. A curfew was in effect for Miami. Every corner of the globe was reckoning with the best version of how to handle and accept this newly realized pandemic.

Instead of rescheduling, Sagal and Geoffrey decided to keep their wedding date, and were married in Sagal's parents' living room wearing their original wedding attire, him in a black tux, her in an ivory satin gown. They posed for photos beneath gold foil balloons reading "MR & MRS" that bobbed above the fireplace mantel behind them.

Afterward, still in their wedding attire, they hit up one of the only places open for food—Trader Joe's. While pushing their cart through the produce section, an employee yelled, through happy tears, "Now that's resilience!"

Sometimes, big love stories turn into small moments.

But love stories will always endure.

And, in the end, love is always— *always*—enough.

Resources

Inspiration

- **100 Layer Cake**, which began as a DIY wedding blog in 2009, is now home to a curated collection of wedding and parenting content.

- **Adventure Instead** is a website run by a team of women that specializes in adventure photography and elopements in Colorado and the Pacific Northwest.

- **Art of Eloping** (brought to you by yours truly) is an inclusive website dedicated to helping couples who want to elope make it a reality. We share couples' stories along with vendors who specialize in elopements and intimate ceremonies.

- **Carats & Cake** connects couples with vendors who are in their area via real weddings they've featured on their site.

- **Hello May** is an Australian-based, unconventional print magazine, blog, and directory connecting vendors with couples in Australia and New Zealand.

- **Love Hard Honey** is an inclusive wedding site that features diverse weddings and elopement inspiration to help couples create their dream weddings.

- **Simply Eloped** offers affordable elopement packages in cities around the US.

- **Wandering Weddings** provides resources and inspiration for couples seeking adventure elopements.

Attire

- **Allure Bridals** offers both couture and ready-to-wear gowns with a focus on beading, floral appliqués, and dramatic backs.

- **BHLDN** is Anthropologie's wedding line that offers a wide selection of curated brands and styles, both online and in stores nationwide.

- **Essense of Australia** offers a huge array of gowns, but where the brand really shines is in its modern take on timeless silhouettes and embellishments.

- **French Knot Couture**—which spawned from an Etsy shop—specializes in short and tea-length wedding dresses, all made-to-measure. They also have a killer selection of black dresses and offer couture dresses too, which are handmade by owner Colleen Thorsen.

- **Juniper James Bridal** is a Boone, North Carolina–based shop featuring vintage wedding dresses that can also be ordered online. Juniper James partners with numerous LGBTQ+ initiatives to better serve this community.

- **Justin Alexander** is for the nostalgic bride who seeks an Old Hollywood vibe—think draped, off-the-shoulder necklines, satin ball gowns, beaded bodices, and delicate cap sleeves.

- **Laure de Sagazan** offers a chic City Hall collection of modern mini dresses and airy skirts.

- **Lost in Paris** uses vintage lace sourced from Europe to create sustainable dresses in both ready-to-wear and custom designs.

- **Odylyne the Celebration** creates free-spirited and ethereal gowns—think ruffled sleeves, cascading trains, and elegant lace capes.

- **Rue de Seine**, based in Australia, is the epitome of modern boho-chic. Plus, all dresses are designed in-house—each by the same seamstress, from start to finish, all under one roof (even the lace).

- **Sarah Seven's** collections range from chic and sophisticated to nontraditional, which includes jumpsuits and mini-dresses.

- **Vow'd** offers stylish dresses at affordable price points and works directly with suppliers to curate a collection of affordable dresses in a wide range of styles and sizes, from 0 to 24W.

- **The White by Vera Wang Collection** is an inexpensive line of the legendary designer's dresses that are widely available at David's Bridal.

Registries

- **Honeyfund** is a free honeymoon registry and cash wedding gift registry all-in-one.

- **With Joy** is an online registry that allows you to link all of your other registries in one place.

- **Zola** offers a registry, planning tools, free wedding websites, and prescreened vendors all in one spot.

Acknowledgments

We are deeply grateful to the vendors who so graciously answered our DMs, connected us with their couples, and took the time to meet for coffee and have their brains picked. You are the backbone of this book, and it truly would not exist without you: Natasha Anakotta, American Marriage Ministries; Cactus Wedding Collective; Emily Clemenson, Veritas Vineyard & Winery; Alexandra Gault, Alex Mari Photography; Olivia Graziano and Zach Murphy, Birds of Passage Co.; Gabrielle Hakman, chef; Samia Jrab of Samia's Studios, photographer and perennial cheerleader of this book; Christine Lupo, jewelry designer; Jeff Maszal, Wedding Ceremonies by Jeff; Lauren Miller, Lauren Louise Collective; Taylor Parker, Taylor Parker Photography; Peggy Picot, Maison Pestea Photography; Kelley Patton, makeup artist; Ashley Peters, The Stylist Abroad; Bonnie Sen, Bonnie Sen Photography; Blair Speed, nighttime photographer extraordinaire; Anne Widdop, founder of Fuze Ceremonies and the best host in Scotland; and Joshua

Kane Wood, photographer and a tremendous help early on.

To the couples who shared the most intimate and personal details of their love stories: thank you. Your sentiments and joy lift this book in ways we couldn't have imagined, and we are deeply indebted to you for your openness in sharing: Haylie Ahart and Kevin McGaughey; Caroline Anderson and Marty Salvi; Katelyn Remington-Arata and Carlos Arata; Lauren Bacon and Lindsay Smith; RaeAnn Brixius Fahnrich and Nick Fahnrich; Erin and Jeff Cannata; Julie Ann Costantino and William "Tripp" Wray III; Chris DiPasquale and Herbie Hickmott; Shelby and Kyle; Bri and Lindsey Leaverton; Amber and Bryan Ford; Elizabeth and RJ Garcia; Lana and Ben Lodge; Amy Morton and Stafford Ward; Acacia and Evan Rowland; Sagal Samantar and Geoffrey Johnson; Deanna Zaccagnini and David Mike.

To Vanessa Price, thank you for providing the expertise only you can offer, with such grace, so late in the game. To Susie Saltzman, your kindness and thoughtfulness in making last-minute contributions buoyed this ship at the last hour. To Candice Coppola, Eleni N. Gage, and Shira Savada, thank you for your invaluable expert input and time over the phone and Zoom—may we meet one day! To Stephen Goldman, Esq., your patience and generosity in taking the time to break down family law and student loans and prenups is beyond appreciated, and to Lisa Kiefer, biggest thanks for connecting us.

Our immense gratitude goes to Lynn Beahan, whose tireless efforts some twenty years ago on the first book paved the way for this one.

A huge thank-you to Kelly Grant and everyone at ALX Community for creating a space to make this a reality, and for believing. Thank you to Maurisa Potts for your early advice and immense support along the way.

To Persephone Maglaya: There are no words significant enough to capture the seismic shift you had and still have on this idea that you believe in so much. Thank you for your clear vision and belief.

Thank you to Caroline Cunningham and Erica Sloan for your instant support when this book was still a kernel of an idea, as well as your deep insight on destinations. Your contributions are remarkable.

To our editor, Claire Gilhuly, who skillfully shaped this book through not only her editorial expertise, but also the indispensable lens of her wedding industry experience: We are forever grateful. Thanks to everyone at Chronicle Books who made this book a reality.

And to our agent, Jane Dystel, who welcomed this book idea and provided constant counsel and support as it took shape: You have our enduring thanks.

From Kim

Thank you to my parents for raising me on books and magazines. Thanks to my brother, Andy, for believing in this idea from the start. To my sister, Jes, thanks for a lifetime of imagination. Margo and Dave Paul, thanks for firing on all eight. To Laura Hayes, thank you for the immense support regarding quitting. To Jen Foley, thank you for the long calls and annual visits. To Maggie Livelsberger, thanks for always checking in and twenty years of friendship, and to Ally for being Ally. Thanks goes to Jen Moritz for your steadfast Pittsburgh friendship. To Rosa Cartagena, Hayley Garrison Phillips, and Jackson Knapp, thank you for the unruly support of the quad. And the biggest thanks of all to Kurtis Paul, for giving me the space to do my thing and not asking any questions.

From Scott

Thank you to Camille, my inspiration and eloping partner. I want to thank Marnie Cochran for patiently explaining how publishing works, and for finding me an agent. Also Lynn Beahan, my co-author on the first book, and Jane Dystel for saying yes (twice!). Most of all, I want to thank Camille for this journey. It was her idea to elope in the first place and she saw no reason why an unpublished author shouldn't write a book on the subject. Her encouragement and support then, and ever since, has made all the difference.